WOWEE ZOW

Praise for the se

It was only a matter of time before a clever publisher realized that there is an audience for whom *Exile on Main Street* or *Electric Ladyland* are as significant and worthy of study as *The Catcher in the Rye* or *Middlemarch* ... The series ... is freewheeling and eclectic, ranging from minute rock-geek analysis to idiosyncratic personal celebration—*The New York Times Book Review*

Ideal for the rock geek who thinks liner notes just aren't enough—*Rolling Stone*

One of the coolest publishing imprints on the planet—*Bookslut*

These are for the insane collectors out there who appreciate fantastic design, well-executed thinking, and things that make your house look cool. Each volume in this series takes a seminal album and breaks it down in startling minutiae. We love these. We are huge nerds—*Vice*

A brilliant series ... each one a work of real love—*NME* (UK)

Passionate, obsessive, and smart—*Nylon*

Religious tracts for the rock 'n' roll faithful—*Boldtype*

[A] consistently excellent series—*Uncut* (UK)

We ... aren't naive enough to think that we're your only source for reading about music (but if we had our way ... watch out). For those of you who really like to know everything there is to know about an album, you'd do well to check out Continuum's "33 1/3" series of books—*Pitchfork*

For reviews of individual titles in the series, please visit our blog at 333sound.com and our website at http://www.bloomsbury.com/musicandsoundstudies

Follow us on Twitter: @333books

Like us on Facebook: https://www.facebook.com/33.3books

For a complete list of books in this series, see the back of this book

For more information about the series, please visit our new blog:

www.333sound.com

Where you'll find:

– Author and artist interviews

– Author profiles

– News about the series

– How to submit a proposal to our open call

– Things we find amusing

Wowee Zowee

Bryan Charles

BLOOMSBURY ACADEMIC
NEW YORK • LONDON • OXFORD • NEW DELHI • SYDNEY

BLOOMSBURY ACADEMIC
Bloomsbury Publishing Inc
1385 Broadway, New York, NY 10018, USA
50 Bedford Square, London, WC1B 3DP, UK
29 Earlsfort Terrace, Dublin 2, Ireland

BLOOMSBURY, BLOOMSBURY ACADEMIC and the Diana logo are
trademarks of Bloomsbury Publishing Plc

First published in 2010 by the Continuum International Publishing
Group Inc
Reprinted by Bloomsbury Academic 2013, 2014, 2015, 2017,
2018 (twice), 2019, 2020, 2021, 2022, 2023

Charles, Bryan.
Wowee Zowee / Bryan Charles.
p. cm.—(33 1/3)
ISBN-13: 978-0-8264-2957-5 (pbk. : alk. paper)
ISBN-10: 0-8264-2957-2 (pbk. : alk. paper) 1. Pavement (Musical
group) 2. Rock musicians—United States—Biography. I. Title.
II. Series.
ML421.P38C53 2010
782.42166092'2—dc22
2009051862

ISBN: PB: 978-0-8264-2957-5
ePDF: 978-1-4411-9875-4
eBook: 978-1-4411-0377-2

Typeset by Pindar NZ, Auckland, New Zealand
Series: 33 1/3, volume 72

Printed and bound in Great Britain

To find out more about our authors and books visit www.bloomsbury.com
and sign up for our newsletters.

Interviews

Gerard Cosloy, May 20 and 21, 2008
Doug Easley, March 18, 2009
Bryce Goggin, April 1, 2009
Danny Goldberg, March 12, 2009
Mark Ibold, March 10, 2009
Scott Kannberg, July 14 and October 10, 2008
Steve Keene, June 7, 2009
Chris Lombardi, June 17, 2008
Stephen Malkmus, May 14 and June 17, 2009
Bob Nastanovich, July 10, 2008 and October 6, 2009
Mark Venezia, April 6, 2009
Steve West, May 27, 2009

I was living in Kalamazoo Michigan on Walwood Place. There was a football field in front of the house. Starting in August the WMU Broncos would practice there. I'd wake to their grunts and whistles and yells. In the winter and spring the field was empty. We'd slip through an opening in the fence and let Spot run around. On a hill overlooking the field was East Hall, part of the old main campus, now barely in use. East Hall was a red brick building with broad white columns. You could see all of Kalamazoo from its steps. The steps were a good place to ponder existential dilemmas. They were a good place to make out. It was early 95. I was twenty years old. I ate Papa John's for dinner two or three nights a week.

The Walwood pad was a former assisted-living facility, two large apartments connected by a back set of service stairs. Greg, Chafe and Curt lived in the upstairs unit. Justin, Spot, Luke and I lived downstairs. Spot was Justin's dalmatian. He was a great-looking dog but a little nuts. He seemed to attack everyone except Justin and me. I'd met Justin a year earlier when we were both music writers at the Western Herald. Justin dug Greil Marcus and Lester Bangs. His criticism was stuffed with non sequiturs and obscure references. I was less sure of myself as a critic and by early 95 I'd essentially quit. I liked writing and playing music more than analyzing and critiquing it.

I played guitar and sang in a band called Fletcher. We were a power trio with a Jawbreaker vibe. I had my Stratocaster and Twin Reverb in the Walwood basement. I spent hours down there writing songs. I'd get blitzed, crank the reverb and play surf tunes. Chafe and Curt were in a quasi-Dischord outfit called Inourselves. Their apartment was littered with instruments and recording machines. Someone was always listening to or playing music in that house. This was in keeping with the Kalamazoo ethos of the time. There were dozens of bands and everyone was a rock dude — whether they actually played music or not. Even the girls were rock dudes. Everyone went to shows and bought vinyl and jocked out on obscure bands. At the same time underground vs. mainstream tensions had eased. Once in a while a big band made a splash. A few months earlier Weezer's first record had hit the city like a megaton blast. It was beloved in all quarters of the fragmenting scene.

Justin worked at Flipside, Kalamazoo's best record store and a haven for rock dudes in the middle of awkward musical transitions. A mini movement was afoot in the local hardcore community. Straight edge fell by the wayside. Darker pleasures reigned. Abstemious emo geeks ditched the gas-station work shirts and sanctimony.

They started to blow grass and roll their own cigarettes. They grooved on jazz and orchestral pop. Moss Icon and Born Against were out. Sun Ra, Captain Beefheart and Brian Wilson were in. A new breed of geek materialized. They'd hang by the vinyl bins at Flipside extolling the genius of hophead jazz greats. There was dietary capitulation. Soy milk and tofu were out. Beer and cheeseburgers were in. The weird change seemed to occur overnight. I was leery of this musically schizoid behavior and regarded the jazz and reefer scene with contempt. As a Flipside employee even Justin — a Beatles freak and all-around power pop guy — was susceptible. He disowned the traditional in favor of screeching free-form noise. He declaimed old favorites to be passé. He boned up on jazz history and held forth on this or that player or this or that famous session. He burned through new trends and passions forever in search of the Next Thing.

One day he came home with some promo CDs. We sat in his room going through them. I got the new Pavement, he said. He put it on. I don't remember what I was thinking as it played. I don't remember if we discussed it or not. All I know is what I heard made no impression on me. We played all or part of the disc. Justin took it off. I didn't think about it again for a long time.

One record I continued to think about was Slanted and Enchanted, Pavement's first album. It was three years old but already felt to me like a timeless classic. I listened to it often that spring and early summer. It was in permanent rotation in a stack of vinyl I hauled back and forth between home and my job at Boogie Records.

My favorite songs were Summer Babe, In the Mouth a Desert and Here. I also liked Conduit for Sale and Zurich Is Stained. I knew little about Pavement. I didn't know who the members were or where they were from. I knew I liked Unseen Power of the Picket Fence — their song on the No Alternative compilation — and I remembered sitting in my dorm room watching MTV and seeing the video for Cut Your Hair. That was a year ago. That had been strange. You saw strange things on MTV then. I saw Jawbox get interviewed by Lewis Largent, the über bland host of 120 Minutes. He asked about the rave scene in Washington DC. They told him they didn't know anything about it. He apologized and admitted it was a stupid question.

Cut Your Hair was the first single off Pavement's second record, Crooked Rain, Crooked Rain. I didn't own it. I don't know how I came to own Slanted and Enchanted. Maybe I bought it on the recommendation of a friend. Maybe it was given to me. Maybe I stole it from Boogie. The store, a former Kalamazoo institution, was in the last lap of a sad fall from grace. The absentee owner was a jerk. He ran it into the ground. He stocked the CD bins with bottom-rung cutouts no one would touch. Employee theft was rampant — more a reaction to the store's mismanagement than a root cause of its downfall. In any event I never bought Crooked Rain. And when the record with the underwhelming promo came out I didn't buy that one either. It was called Wowee Zowee. I never heard any singles. No one I knew talked it up.

Fletcher went into the studio to cut songs for a seven-inch. A month later we went out on a weeklong

tour. Most of our shows were in the basements or living rooms of punk houses. In Baltimore we played at a
converted strip club with a pole still in the center of the
stage. The only people there were the guys in the band
we played with. I liked playing live but didn't like touring.
I didn't like breaking my routines or being away from my
shit. I didn't like staying up late drinking beer with strangers. I didn't like sleeping on floors or in the back of the
van. Paul — the bass player and my best friend — loved
it. He could have gone out for months at a time. I can still
see him nursing a forty and gassing about music in Kent
Ohio or Paramus New Jersey or Knoxville Tennessee.

One thing I didn't mind about touring was the long
drives. We each brought a bunch of tapes. It was nice
to listen to music and watch the road or stare out at
the landscape and highway scenes. Dan the drummer
brought Crooked Rain, Crooked Rain. We played it a
lot. It was the first time I'd ever spent any time with it.
Crooked Rain was great driving music. Many of the songs
have a sunny and open quality — not least Cut Your Hair
and its ooh-ooh-ooh-ooh-ooh-ooh chorus. But there's
also an undercurrent of melancholy on the record, on
slow songs like Stop Breathin and Heaven Is a Truck.
Then there are times when the two aesthetics collide and
merge perfectly, as on Gold Soundz and Range Life, slow
to midtempo numbers whose chords and lyrics evoke a
wonderful mix of both possibility and resignation. *Is it a
crisis or a boring change when it's central, so essential? It has
a nice ring when you laugh at the lowlife opinions . . . Out on
my skateboard the night is just humming and the gum smacks
are a pulse I follow, if my Walkman fades I got absolutely no*

one, no one but myself to blame. They were good songs to listen to in a van on the road far from home.

The following spring I began dating a girl named Elise. She was beautiful, promiscuous, paranoid, insecure. She shoplifted compulsively and snorted crushed Ritalin. I knew all this beforehand but went for her anyway. I was reading a lot of Hemingway and saw myself as Jake Barnes — stoic in the face of moral and cultural disorder and possessed of great depth. I thought my life was boring and wanted my own Lady Brett.

Elise had been living in a house on Academy Street but had trashed her room on a pill binge and been kicked out. Now she lived with her parents in Indiana and worked part-time at a hotel. She stole credit card numbers from customer receipts and used them to place daily long-distance calls to me. She was often high when we talked and her banter was strange. Once she called from a payphone at work and talked of nothing but a lighted exit sign in the lobby. The sign was having some kind of wild effect on her. I tried to get off the phone. She had a minor meltdown. All right, I said and listened for another hour. We exchanged long letters in which we cast ourselves as doomed figures too sensitive for the world. Elise sent provocative photo-booth strips. I grooved on the drama and braced for trouble, imagined answering the phone to a hostile inquiry — I found this number on my credit card bill, who the hell are you? Such a call never came. Elise continued her nutty gabfests.

I'd signed on for the swing shift at the paper mill. I was making nice bread but perpetually exhausted. Work you don't believe in or love is a waste of life. I'd had inklings of this before. I was dead certain of it now. I was a few steps closer to the endless disappointments and compromises of the adult world.

One night on the eleven-to-seven a weird feeling came over me. My breathing became labored. Everything seemed far away. The paper machine roared. It was the size of a city block — a howling unstoppable beast. One wrong move and it could maim or kill me. I emptied the broke boxes — huge waste-paper bins — which required a forklift. I'd driven them dozens of times but was scared to be on one now. What if I crashed and the forklift tipped over? The fucking thing would crush me and that'd be the end. It was eighty and humid outside and much hotter in the mill, probably over a hundred degrees. I was dripping sweat, nauseous, already spent. I found the foreman and told him I was sick. I walked out to the parking lot and sat in my car. A few minutes later I was able to breathe again.

Back home there were people drinking beer on the porch. I decided I couldn't face that scene either. I called Elise and told her I wanted to drive to her place tonight. Okay, she said in a sleepy voice. I threw some clothes in a bag and hit I-94. I pulled off at a truck stop and wolfed a greasy one a.m. meal. I hit I-69 and cruised south for three hours. The window was down. Warm air rushed in. My car only had a radio. I scanned through the stations. I landed on Pretty Noose by Soundgarden two or three times. I sang along at the top of my lungs.

The shift cycle had turned over. I had the next few days off. I stayed with Elise, sleeping on a twin bed in her little brother's old room. My body was out of whack from working the swing shift. I was pale and tired and felt older than twenty-one. The days in Indiana were relaxing. Elise and I went to the movies. We ate at Waffle & Steak. We walked around Meijer's Thrifty Acres. We watched TV. We screwed in her bathroom after her folks went to bed. In Broad Ripple one night we stopped at a record store. I was flipping through the used vinyl, saw a copy of Wowee Zowee and paused. Something compelled me to take it out of the bin. It was a double LP with a gatefold cover. The cover was an abstract painting of two strange figures sitting next to a dog. Pavement? said one of the figures. Wowee Zowee! thought the dog. On the back were individual photos of the band under the words Sordid Sentinels. Aside from dim memories of the Cut Your Hair and Range Life videos — which I'd seen one or two times each — this was the first time I really saw what the band looked like. One of them was in a bubble bath smiling, holding a Racing Form. One wore sunglasses and had what looked like black wax smushed in his teeth. One was a ghostly disembodied head floating inside a TV. Two were pictured eating. Beneath the photos was a crude doodle of a wizard with a thought bubble that said Pavement ist Rad! Inside the gatefold hand-scrawled text bordered a large drawing resembling a system of interlocking freeways. Dick-Sucking Fool at Pussy-Licking School it said at the top. I chuckled at that and read some of the text. I kept the record with me as I browsed some more. I inspected it again then brought it up to the counter. What possessed me to buy it? I'll never know. I had no overwhelming urge to give Wowee Zowee another chance. I hadn't even listened to

Pavement lately. Maybe it was the fact that it was used and I had the money and was itching to spend a few bucks. Maybe it was vinyl fetishism and I was drawn to the big art and the gatefold. Either way I paid for it and we left. When I got home I shelved it in the P section and never took it out once.

At the end of the summer I borrowed Paul's van and drove to Indiana. Elise and I loaded her things and she moved back to Kalamazoo. She got a job as a waitress at Blake's Diner and found a room in a house on Vine Street with two speed freaks. One of them worked at the Subway on campus. I'd been ordering sandwiches from him for years. He worked incredibly quickly with an odd machine-like precision. He could assemble a boss footlong in seconds without asking you to repeat any part of your order. Paul and I had always marveled at his technique. Now it made sense.

Fall passed into winter. Things with Elise went downhill. She grew increasingly hostile, jealous of everyone I talked to. Yet she flirted openly — pathologically — with other men. In December I broke up with her. She started screwing another dude immediately. I walked to her pad in a fury and crashed their post-pork cuddle fest. I dumped a box of her shit on the back porch. I yelled at her window till the light came on. Elise opened the door. I looked in the window and saw the dude in her bed. He was wearing a blue T-shirt and had a hand pressed to his forehead. That one visual was too much for me. Elise and I got back together. We clung to each other out of spite.

I was living in the upstairs Walwood apartment now with Paul and Trish. We had a dinner party one night.

Paul's mom was in town. Trish made eggplant parmesan and tiramisu. Elise flipped out after a glass of wine and sat babbling incoherently. We tried talking around her. It didn't work. Finally she rose from the table, stumbled to my room and passed out. Paul was fed up. He'd never liked Elise and didn't want her around. Trish didn't mind kicking back with a cocktail and listening to Elise rant. I like her, said Trish, she's entertaining.

Entertaining, yes. She'd called me crying, threatening suicide. She'd drop by at odd times, uninvited, spewing venomous remarks. She snuck into the pad when no one was there and wrote the word *home* on the wall over my bed in her own blood. She had body image issues. She didn't eat. Or she'd binge eat and puke. Or binge eat and snarf laxatives till her asshole was chapped. We'd always had good sex. Now even that appalled me. As did her living situation. The speed freaks unnerved me. Their crib was lightless, smoke-filled, depressing. I went there infrequently and used the back door when I did. Except for this one day when I used the front door and paused in the living room and by chance looked down. There behind an old recliner was a stack of CDs. On top of the stack was Pavement's Brighten the Corners. Their fourth LP. It had just come out. It was strange to see it there. I didn't think either of the speed freaks liked indie rock. I scoped the other CDs. It was a random assortment — no other indie bands. Most likely someone had left the Pavement CD there by accident or the whole stack was stolen and one of the speed freaks was going to try and sell it back.

— Whose CDs are these?

— I don't know, said Elise. — Why?

— You think anyone would mind if I took this?

— What is it?

— The new Pavement album.

— Pavement?

— Yeah.

— Go ahead and take it.

I went home and played it. I liked it at once. The lyrics blew my mind. They sounded like poetry. They were typed in the insert and read like poetry too. *Glance, don't stare, soon you're being told to recognize your heirs . . . Cherish your memorized weakness, fashioned from a manifesto . . . If my soul has a shape well then it is an ellipse and this slap is a gift . . . Open call for the prison architects, send me your blueprints ASAP.* The music was straightforward, played more or less cleanly. But there was a playfulness, a humor, a skillful balance of light and dark that I found lacking in most things — literature as well as rock music. The production was different from Slanted and Enchanted and Crooked Rain. Those records had a rawness and the performances weren't as tight. They'd been labeled lo-fi. I never quite saw them that way. Early Sebadoh was lo-fi, obviously recorded on two tape players. So to a lesser extent were Bee Thousand and Alien Lanes, Guided by Voices' two mid-90s breakouts. Slanted and Crooked Rain couldn't be called overproduced. But they were recorded artfully enough that the lo-fi tag seemed lazy to me. Still, the Brighten the Corners production was unquestionably more polished. The liner notes said it was co-recorded by Mitch Easter, who'd worked on the first few R.E.M. records. The association made sense. Unseen Power of the Picket Fence is explicitly about R.E.M.'s early days and Pavement had covered — gently reconfigured — one of my favorite R.E.M. tunes, Camera. The Easter sound was well suited to the Brighten the Corners material. The album has a warm organic feel — like Chronic Town and Murmur, two of my all-time faves.

I listened to Brighten the Corners nonstop. I bought it on vinyl even though I had the CD. I played the vinyl in my room, the CD in the bathroom boombox while I showered and kept a dubbed cassette copy in my Walkman at all times. One day I ran into Justin. He asked what I'd been listening to lately. The new Pavement, I said, it's fucking awesome. Yeah I don't know, I'm not into it, he said. He mocked the part in Shady Lane that goes *oh my god* over and over. There'd been two hundred Next Things since Slanted and Enchanted. Built to Spill was hot shit now. Modest Mouse was coming up. Justin and the jazz geeks thought Wilco was boss. I liked that stuff too. But not like I liked Brighten the Corners. I played it and sang from it so often Paul and Trish knew the words. I began to view my life through the lens of its songs. Elise would be on the floor of my room sobbing, I'd hear Shady Lane in my head. *You're so beautiful to look at when you cry.* I'd ponder life after college and my dreams of being a writer and scattered Brighten the Corners lyrics would flit through my daydreams. *I'm my only critic . . . The language of influence is cluttered with hard Cs . . . I trust you will tell me if I am making a fool of myself.* Sometime later I found out Elise had cheated on me and we broke up for good. I packed her stuff into my Subaru and drove her back to Indiana and all the way down on I-69 under a late-May sky Transport Is Arranged played on an internal loop. *I know you're my lady but I could trickle, I could flood, a voice coach taught me to sing, he couldn't teach me to love.* We unloaded her shit. I left her standing in the driveway. I sped back to Michigan. The sun set halfway there. A depressive sort of lightness flooded my heart. Pavement addressed this complex emotional paradox. *I need to get born, I need to get dead.* The radio played ten-minute blocks of commercials. It played AC/DC. It played the Verve Pipe. It played Sublime.

It was now summer 97. I was a college graduate, scared shitless of the future, unemployed. I had a few hundred bucks saved and didn't look for a job. I stayed in the apartment reading, writing, playing guitar. I took long walks around Kalamazoo listening to Brighten the Corners, Slanted and Enchanted, Crooked Rain, the four-song Watery, Domestic EP. I'd liked those records before. They were miraculous now. I listened to Pavement to the exclusion of all other bands. I saw them as one of the defining forces of my life.

The funny thing was I never played Wowee Zowee. It was there on the shelf with the other records, untouched. I still had dim memories of that first time I'd heard it, the lack of excitement I felt. I had a sense too that the record was a failure somehow, not as good as the rest. I don't know where I got this. Maybe a friend told me or maybe it was mentioned in some of the Brighten the Corners press. By press I mean whatever would have appeared in Spin or Rolling Stone. Those were the only rock mags I read and aside from word of mouth they were my only means of keeping up. I didn't have cable or own a computer. I'd only been on the Internet a handful of times and wasn't really sure what to do on there anyway.

My bread ran out. Paul and Trish floated me. For lack of other options or ideas I became a substitute teacher. Starting in September I woke each morning at six to call the sub service and see if they had work. I took every assignment they offered me — kindergarten through high school, auto shop to math. Some days there was nothing and I stayed home and wrote. It was nice to have money coming in but every dime was accounted for. There was no room in the budget for treats. Then I heard Pavement was coming to Grand Rapids. They were playing at the Intersection, a relatively small club. I agonized over the matter for two or three days. Recently I'd gotten a credit card. The first thing I bought with it was a bag of Doritos at a gas station on the way to a Radiohead concert — itself an extravagance that still caused me great guilt. The second thing was a computer. It cost twelve hundred bucks. Owing that money terrified me. I thought about it constantly. It seemed I'd never be able to pay it back. And that was the least of it. There was also twenty grand in student loans. I was starting my adult life with a low-paying place-holder job, already drowning in debt. I decided I wouldn't charge another cent to my credit card till I'd paid at least some of it down. That meant if I wanted to see Pavement I'd have to pay cash, of which I had almost none. It's strange to think about it now — three days of deliberations over whether or not to spend twelve dollars to see my favorite band play a small club. In the end I took the plunge. I bought a ticket at Repeat the Beat. I walked out feeling happy, thinking of what songs I wanted to hear.

The night of the show I drove a few people up to Grand Rapids. We rolled in early and hit Yesterdog for a snack. Everyone munched hot dogs but me. I'd eaten beforehand and sat nursing a water. I was trying to recoup some of the money I was giving up not taking a subbing gig the next day. The Intersection was crowded. A girl I had a crush on named Chrissy was there. She was dating a handsome cipher I'd nicknamed Plastic Man. He was nowhere around. I sat across from her and tried sending vibrations. She either didn't notice or didn't care. After a while I got up and walked through the crowd. I stopped and stood near the front of the stage. Soon the house lights went down. Pavement walked out. A guy next to me was shouting.

— Where's Malkmus? he said.

I wasn't sure who this was.

— There he is! There's Malkmus!

I looked at the stage. A tall thin man with brown hair had come out. He strapped on a guitar and approached the microphone. He scratched his nose and said something about his allergies.

— No shit! yelled the guy next to me.

— It's great to be here in central Michigan, said Malkmus. His voice was flat. He didn't sound thrilled.

— It's western! Western Michigan! yelled the guy.

Malkmus looked at the yelling man.

— Whatever, he said.

— This is a tune called Grounded, he said.

The band launched into a slow number I didn't

recognize. The guitar notes were clean and high and pretty. I ticked through the catalog. It had to be on Wowee Zowee. Hours later in my room I took that record from the shelf. Sure enough Grounded was on the first side. I played it. When it was over I lifted the needle and started the record from the beginning. It was late. The house was quiet. Paul was at work and Trish was asleep. I had the volume down low. I entered a sort of dream state. Wowee Zowee went through me like a blast of pure light.

Nine years later I was living in New York City. I walked out of the subway into Union Square. I entered the Virgin Megastore looking to kill some time. Near the front of the store was a table stacked with little books. They had album covers on the front and were named for the album they featured. I picked one up and looked through it — Unknown Pleasures or Doolittle. It seemed to be entirely about that one record, with bits of the band's history thrown in. I scanned the rest of the table and looked through a few other books. I read the list of available and upcoming titles. I didn't see one for Pavement. How could that be? R.E.M., Pixies, the Replacements — Guided by Voices and Nirvana coming soon. Surely there was one in the hopper for Pavement. Or maybe there wasn't. My pulse started to quicken. I thought, you'll be the one. Within a few seconds I had the whole thing mapped out. I'd do Slanted and Enchanted, their epochal first LP. A record that defined — no, invented — modern indie rock. Endlessly imitated, never surpassed. Let's be honest — never even equaled. I stood daydreaming at the table. Music blared through the store. I imagined a little book with Slanted and Enchanted on the cover, my name underneath. I'd place the record in context. Early 92 — a revolution prophesied. Alternative music as commercially viable. I'd break it down song by song, examine every lyric, drum fill, guitar lick. I'd argue against the notion of Pavement as slackers, banish that dead concept once and for all. And here was the best thing — I'd talk to the band. What would I ask them? I hadn't the faintest idea. My first novel was coming out soon. I'd started a second one. I'd knock that out and then write the Pavement book. Everything was so fucking groovy. I was shaking almost. I left the Virgin store and went to the movies. Halfway through the previews I forgot about the little books.

My bankroll thinned. I got a temp gig at Virgin Records doing sub-intern shit. My boss was sixty but dressed like she was sixteen. I made Starbucks runs for her. I answered the phone. I ordered office supplies. I did people's expenses. I sat with a spreadsheet reading cellphone-provider websites, checking to see if Fat Joe/ Meatloaf/Janet Jackson/30 Seconds to Mars ringtones were on sale. 30 Seconds to Mars was a top priority at Virgin. The actor Jared Leto was their songwriter and frontman. Leto thought he was a genius. Leto was dead fucking wrong. His band was pure shit. People in the office acted like they were the Rolling Stones. The same two 30 Seconds to Mars singles played loudly at all times. Leto was given enormous sums to make big-budget videos that aped Kubrick's The Shining and Bertolucci's

The Last Emperor. He was praised in meetings for his dedication to his craft. One guy said to me, you know Jared doesn't have to be doing this, he turned down a starring role in that Clint Eastwood movie about Iwo Jima so he could go on tour, you have to admire that.

Work on my second novel stalled. By then the first one had been out for three months. There were certain emotional rewards but its presence in the world generally hadn't changed my life. I needed something to pin my hopes on. The Pavement book filled the void. There'd been a shift in my thinking. Slanted and Enchanted was no longer the one. It seemed too obvious somehow. Plenty had been written about it before. It always shows up on lists — best of the 90s, best indie records etc. I mulled it over in my cubicle as down the hall Leto wailed. What about Crooked Rain, Crooked Rain? The album that spawned the closest thing Pavement had to a hit and delivered them to the brink of big mainstream success. It was a promising notion. Crooked Rain's context was heady. It came out in February of 94. A sea change was coming. We just didn't know it. Then early April, the death of Kurt Cobain, his demons revealed. Depression, white horse, the dark side of fame. Grunge kids coast to coast weeping. Me in a quivering heap on my dorm room floor. Middlebrow rock writers drawing Lennon comparisons. Nirvana gets a huge sales bump. Commerce prevails. The alt-rock juggernaut rolls on. Smashing Pumpkins headline Lollapalooza, still in Siamese Dream mode. Billy Corgan's multicolored hippie shirts and thinning hair — a year away from the Zero shirt, the god complex, the shaved dome. The curtain thrown back. Bush's Sixteen Stone hits the scene — their tune Little Things a cunt hair away from outright Teen Spirit plagiarism. Alternative music as merely another product. Après Kurt the deluge. A revolution denied.

My next thought was Terror Twilight, Pavement's fifth and final LP. Practically a Stephen Malkmus solo effort. Somber in tone, a Nigel Godrich production, lots of reverb and space blips. Terror Twilight closed out the decade and in effect my adolescence. In March of 99 — three months before its release — I entered my first Wall Street cubicle sporting a hand-me-down suit and tie. By November of that year the band was effectively done. But the story of their passive-aggressive dissolution was a downer. I decided I had no interest in chronicling Pavement's demise. That's when it hit me. You're overlooking the obvious. Wowee Zowee — your favorite record of all time.

You shrugged it off initially. Returned to it later. When you did it blew your mind. You think probably others share this experience. Early resistance followed by rabid embrace. Wowee Zowee is a wild, unpredictable record. Fragmented, impressionistic, casually brilliant. Brilliance revealed in stages. Sprawling. Eighteen disparate songs that somehow magically cohere. Maybe a little aloof at first but once you spend a little time with it it keeps giving back to you. Potentially larger theme: Wowee Zowee's anarchic form as career calculation. Pavement coming close to the Big Time, sensing danger, showing fear or disgust, taking a hundred steps back. You've heard this theory before. You're not sure where. But hey, you're easily swayed. You could be convinced of this. Back in the 90s you didn't think of indie — or any current rock music — as art. That seemed to be a designation for old classics. The Beatles made art. Bob Dylan made art. Pink Floyd, with their synth-heavy concept albums, made art. Now you know better. Pavement made art. There's no question about this. Wowee Zowee is an artful and beautiful record. It has made you laugh, moved you to tears and pretty much everything in between. It took some knocks in its day but is now regarded as one of their best — even by many hardcore fans as *the* best. Ergo your thesis: underdog record greeted with head-wags and confusion stands the test of time to become fan favorite and indie rock classic.

You've never owned it on CD. On your lunch break you buy a copy of the just-released Wowee Zowee reissue, a double-disc set featuring Peel Sessions, b-sides, other assorted extra tracks. You commandeer a yellow pad from the Virgin supply closet and begin making notes. This is among your last acts as an employee of the dying and wretched label. You give your four-days' notice. Your boss hits back with some cold truth: this saves us a tough talk, I was going to let you go anyway.

With your newfound freedom you try to resuscitate your novel. The work goes slowly. Why is this your destiny, this constant spinning of wheels? You think often of Wowee Zowee. The record is so much a part of you — you've heard it so many times — you're pretty sure you can play it from start to finish in your mind. The first note of the first song is a lonesome plucked E string — but wait! What was it like before, when you didn't know any of it? What was it like hearing those songs for the first time? What was it like — shit. Might as well try conjuring prenatal memories. Early impressions and recollections dissipate as you strain for them.

You rotate to Michigan for the holidays then back to New York. You've hit rock bottom money-wise. You borrow a grand from your parents. Your girlfriend springs for meals. You write a Wowee Zowee book proposal and submit it without high hopes. A job offer materializes: proofreading at a financial company, sixty grand a year. You swore you'd never again work in a financial office but have no choice but to accept. You dust off your Brooks Brothers suit and make the midtown scene. You suffer the riffs of your coworkers in the hallways, the elevator, the men's room. The woman in the next cubicle has a radio on her desk. Gwen Stefani's The Sweet Escape plays every hour. In the afternoons she tunes in to Sean Hannity. A web-design creep sits in an office across the aisle. He eschews the overhead lighting in favor of a specially purchased floor lamp. He likes to close the door and blast NPR-approved alt rock — as if playing Gnarls Barkley at a financial firm somehow mitigates the dress code. Work on your novel stalls. You sit stupefied in your cubicle. The hours crawl. You're permanently spent. Back-burner those dreams, son. No — hold on to a little something. Wowee Zowee can save you. You get the green light. Welcome aboard, write the book. You whip out the old yellow pad with renewed vigor, make notes on company time. You fill page after page, barely lifting the pen. You ponder the vagaries of Wowee Zowee and the Pavement legacy as a whole. Yet the more you think about the record the more elusive it becomes, the less certain you are of what you want to say. You reread your notes and press on. You fill up the yellow pad, hit the supply closet for a fresh one. You search for and print dozens of Pavement reviews, interviews, profiles. Other people's words and opinions get jumbled up in your head. You consult rock dude friends — you hang with fewer of them now but they're around. You listen to the records, starting with the Slay Tracks single and going all the way through Terror Twilight. You do all this and still feel lost. The first little flickers of anxiety arrive, the first whiffs of self-doubt. Look at you. What a fraud. You lack the vocabulary for this. You're not a Pitchfork guy — Pitchfork people are all over these books, pushing their theories, arguments, assertions. Interview Pavement? That's a yuk. Given the length and depth of your fandom will you even be able to form words? For years you admired Stephen Malkmus to the point of worship. Now imagine calling him up on the phone. Why'd you want to do this again? What is the point? To explicate the mystery of Wowee Zowee? Talk about a fool's errand. Mystery is essential to the record's very appeal. Why try and crack the code? Why — you look up. Your boss is walking this way. You lay down your pen. He stops at your cubicle. He raps a line of office jive — something about a mandatory interdepartmental initiative. He hands you a paper. He wants you to write out your goals for the year then come to his office and discuss them. Goals? Well sure. Let's see. You've got some pretty big goddamn goals. First on the list is finishing your novel. You've been working on it the last year and a half and are still light years from hitting a groove.

Second is starting the Wowee Zowee book. Yes but ha ha — that's not what he means by goals. He means your goals as a proofreader of financial-marketing brochures, reports, presentations. He walks away. You stare at the paper. Months pass. A year.

Stephen Malkmus and Scott Kannberg were childhood friends. They grew up in Stockton California in the 80s. Certain scenes were exploding. West Coast hardcore. College rock. These were the ancient days of having to seek out the good shit, of talking to friends and strangers to find out what they were into, of visiting the record store weekly in search of cool new or old bands.

There was a bit of a punk scene in Stockton. Stephen played in a hardcore band called the Straw Dogs. They lasted about a year. Stephen graduated high school. He split for the University of Virginia. He returned to Stockton the next summer. He and Scott formed Bag O' Bones. Echo and the Bunnymen and New Order were influences. Stephen sang. The drummer didn't dig his voice. Bag O' Bones stuck to instrumentals. They hooked up some gigs. They played a wedding reception. Someone pulled the plug after three songs. Bag O' Bones was short-lived. Stephen rotated east. Scott did a year at Arizona State. It wasn't quite his scene. He didn't go back.

At UVA Stephen made some new pals. He met David Berman at a Cure concert in Washington DC. A while after that he met Bob Nastanovich. Malkmus, Berman and Nastanovich were rock dudes. They went to shows and bought vinyl and jocked out on obscure bands. They were DJs at the college radio station, WTJU. They got turned on to all kinds of new shit. They formed a noise rock outfit called Ectoslavia. David eventually took control of the group. He gave Stephen and Bob the heave-ho. Stephen played in a couple other bands — Lake Speed and Potted Meat Product. He graduated college. He rolled back to Stockton. It was 1988. Bush One was ascendant. Stephen and Scott met up and started to jam. They both played guitar. Stephen did most of the singing. They made a lot of noise but had some decent tunes too. They decided to record and release their own single. They looked into studios. This dude Gary Young ran one out of his house. Gary was older. He was sort of fried. He'd recorded a bunch of Stockton punk bands. His rates were cheap. Stephen and Scott booked time. In January of 89 they recorded some songs. Gary was a drummer and ended up playing a bit. The result was a four-song seven-inch called Slay Tracks (1933–1969). It came out on their own Treble Kicker label. They pressed a thousand copies. Scott sent some out to the fanzines for review. Slay Tracks had a stark yellow cover. It was hard to know at first glance if the band was Treble Kicker or Pavement. The insert made no mention of anyone named Stephen Malkmus or Scott Kannberg. The main players were listed as S.M. and Spiral Stairs.

Slay Tracks pulled in some good fanzine reviews.

Vinyl geeks and rock dudes sought it out. Dan Koretsky was one of them. Dan lived in Chicago and worked at a record distributor. He ordered two hundred copies of Slay Tracks. Dan was starting a label with his friend Dan Osborn. He wrote Scott a letter saying they wanted to put a Pavement record out. They were also talking to this New York band Royal Trux. Dan and Scott kept in touch. Stephen was traveling abroad. When he rotated stateside he and Scott started to jam. They went back to Gary's and recorded more songs. Koretsky and Osborn's label Drag City was up and running. Pavement's second EP — Demolition Plot J-7 — was Drag City's second release. Pavement got more good reviews. Word continued to spread. They returned to Gary's and laid down more tracks. The new material came out on ten-inch vinyl — the Perfect Sound Forever EP.

Stephen rotated permanently east. He got an apartment in Jersey City with Bob Nastanovich and David Berman. He got a job as a security guard at the Whitney Museum. A small Pavement tour was arranged. In August of 90 Gary and Scott flew to New York. Minimal rehearsals were undertaken. Gary was proving to be a wild card. He was a longtime alcoholic. His playing could be incredible or all over the map. Bob was all set to roadie for the tour. Stephen pulled him aside and said, you better get a couple drums, you know how to keep time. So Bob played second percussion live. He kept a steady beat when Gary was in his cups. They finished the tour. Gary and Scott flew home. An idea had been hatched — let's make a full-length album.

The sessions went down at Gary's pad around

Christmas. They recorded a huge batch of songs in about a week total. Stephen returned to New York. Stephen and Scott assessed the material. They dubbed some tapes and sent them around to independent labels. Those tapes got dubbed and passed around some more. A bunch of people heard it and went apeshit. Drag City released a single featuring three of the new songs. The a-side was a beautiful pop tune called Summer Babe. The first two words of the song were *ice baby*. Reviled white rapper Van Winkle gets a nod. In August of 91 they did another east coast tour. They had a permanent bass player now, a friend of Stephen and Bob's from the New York scene named Mark Ibold. Interest in Pavement and their unreleased record was off the charts. A New York label called Matador vied to put the thing out. Before that happened it received a glowing full-page review in Spin, a review based solely on an unlabeled tape.

Slanted and Enchanted officially came out in March of 92. It was a critical fave and steady seller. Pavement popped up on major-label radars. The band pushed it full-throttle. They recorded some more. They toured the US and Europe. They honed their live skills and got fucking good. They went from playing before a max crowd of twelve hundred opening for My Bloody Valentine in New York to thirty thousand people opening for Nirvana at the Reading Festival — the famous one where Kurt came out in a wheelchair and hospital gown and rocked everyone's face off. Kurt was a Pavement fan. Kurt's fandom could open doors. Seemingly any band he mentioned in passing or advertised on a T-shirt got a lucrative major-label deal. You've heard it before and maybe lived through it. It bears repeating: the early 90s were an insane fucking time.

Gary's drinking worsened. His performances suffered. His wild-man antics irked others in the band. Back in Stockton they tried to demo new songs. Gary was building a new studio but it wasn't done. He was hitting the sauce and couldn't perform. They split for more shows abroad. Tensions escalated. Last-straw scenarios emerged. By the time they rotated stateside Gary and Pavement were quits.

A new drummer had already been more or less picked out. He'd worked as a guard at the Whitney with Stephen and was high school friends with Bob. His name was Steve too but he often went by his last name — West. West lived in a loft in Williamsburg Brooklyn. He had his drums set up there and he and Stephen would jam. Stephen heard about a dude who was building his own recording studio in Manhattan. The guy was called Walleye and worked at Rogue Music, a vintage equipment store located in the same space. A mutual friend approached Walleye and said, I know this band, they're looking to do an album, what do you think? Walleye was hesitant. His studio wasn't quite there yet. But Stephen checked it out and said it'd be fine. Scott flew to New York. Pavement — minus Bob — convened at Walleye's studio, which he'd named Random Falls. Bob was now living in Louisville Kentucky. He was a part of the live show. It seemed unnecessary for him to be in New York to record. Random Falls was on the eighth floor of a building on West Thirtieth Street. It was dark and cramped, still being assembled as they went along. But

Walleye tricked the place out with ace gear from the shop. He brought in vintage amps and microphones and gave the band free rein.

Everyone was excited by the quality of the new songs. There were positive signs on the business end too. Matador was glued up with Atlantic Records. It was kind of a new thing. They now had major-label cash and distribution. Crooked Rain, Crooked Rain seemed poised for bigger things. Around the time it came out Stephen booked another session with Walleye at Random Falls. Stephen, West and Mark recorded a handful of songs. They were spazzier and stranger than the ones on the new record. There was no real plan for what would happen with them.

Now the myth-making begins — mixed in with some truth. The deal with Atlantic paid off. Crooked Rain blew up. Cut Your Hair hit radio and MTV. It was so catchy with that wordless bubblegum chorus. It hit the Billboard modern rock chart. The song itself addressed the crazy music scene. *Bands start up each and every day, I saw another one just the other day, a special new band.* The video was charmingly low-budget: the Pavement guys in a barber shop taking turns in the chair. It turned out these dudes whose album art didn't include their pictures or even their names were handsome, funny, charismatic. The rock world took notice. Major labels began salivating. People in offices drew up contracts. The A&R call went out: sign this band. Meanwhile Pavement ground it out on the road. They toured Europe. They toured the states. During one grueling stretch they played something like fifty-five shows in fifty-two days. Some towns they'd play an all-ages show and an adult show. They rotated to LA and played Cut Your Hair on the Tonight Show. Their fan base grew. A second single was released, Gold Soundz. It was more wistful than Cut Your Hair — *so drunk in the August sun and you're the kind of girl I like because you're empty and I'm empty*. People said Pavement's gonna be huge. They're that phantom thing, the Next Nirvana. It had been three years since Nevermind. It seemed like a fucking eternity — a time/space continuum Cobain himself now occupied.

A lone voice dissented, a literal whine. It belonged to Billy Corgan of Smashing Pumpkins. Corgan still had that innocent twinkle in his eye but was showing signs of the hubris that would characterize his downfall. Corgan was pissed about the Crooked Rain song Range Life, the one that went *out on tour with the Smashing Pumpkins, nature kids, I/they don't have no function, I don't understand what they mean and I could really give a fuck*. Corgan always wanted to be huge. He made no bones about that. But about the only thing he had on Kurt success-wise was that he'd porked Courtney Love first. Now Cobain was ashes. An alt-god vacuum opened up. Corgan was willing — eager — to assume the mantle. He was an egotist with a psyche of jiffy-popping insecurities. He didn't like people who didn't get where he was coming from. He didn't like people saying they could give a fuck what he meant. Early on there'd been talk Pavement would play Lollapalooza — with Smashing Pumpkins headlining. Billy pulled rank. He said no way, I'm not playing with Pavement. Those guys are sarcastic. They're not in this for real. They don't write personal, emotional music.

They don't make WIDESCREEN ART like me. Billy spilled his beef to the festival brass. He recommended bands he thought would be better. Siamese Dream was a multiplatinum hit. Crooked Rain sales were a blip by comparison. Billy conflated humor with carelessness and units moved with artistic achievement. In the end he got his way. Pavement was shitcanned from the bill.

They toured on their own for the rest of the year. West locked in on drums. Bob's role expanded. Pavement was road-tested and stable in a way they'd never been. They left other forms of employment behind. Rock and roll was now their full-time occupation.

Crooked Rain was barely eight months old. Pavement had toured almost constantly for the last two years. Still, they figured now was the time to record a follow-up. The band booked time at Easley Recording in Memphis. Doug Easley and Davis McCain, a couple laid-back cats with deep roots in the local scene, ran the board there. Lately they'd been working with a lot of indie bands. Pavement traveled to Memphis and began to sort out and record new material. They worked quickly and the songs piled up. When they weren't working they grooved on Memphis and snarfed local grub. They recorded an astonishing number of tracks — the Easley session lasted only ten days. A few of the songs had been attempted for Crooked Rain but rerecorded in Memphis. The Memphis versions were radically superior. Walleye was a good guy and he came through with tight pieces. But the Easley guys were total pros. They'd been doing this shit since the Big Star days. Some of the songs they put to tape were already live staples. They'd been in Pavement setlists for a year or more. Also floating around were the songs they'd done with Walleye earlier that year. Those tunes had a different feel. They were more off the cuff. There'd been no plan for them. Now there was. Stephen wanted them on this record too.

Pavement wrapped up at Easley. They mixed the tracks and recorded overdubs in New York. They took a step back and assessed the material. It was a wild scene. They had fully fleshed-out songs and whispers and rumors of half-formed ones. They had songs that followed a hard-to-gauge internal logic, sometimes drifting into the ether or flying totally off the rails, sometimes achieving an unlikely resolution. They had punk tunes and country tunes and sad tunes and funny ones. They had fuzzy pop and angular new wave. They had raunchy guitar solos and stoner blues. They had pristine jangle and pedal steel. The final track list ran to eighteen songs and filled three sides of vinyl. Side four was blank. There was an empty thought bubble on the label. The record's title was a nod to Gary. He'd say wowee zowee when something blew his mind.

Major labels were still hounding them, offering them big dough. It was the waning days of a golden era but righteous coin could still be had. The Jesus Lizard was on Capitol. Royal Trux — Pavement's old Drag City label mate — was on Virgin. Who had made these decisions? Who thought these weird fucking bands would recoup? Pavement weighed their options. They decided against signing a big contract. What was the difference anyway? Matador still trucked with a major. The Atlantic deal was history. They were with Warner Brothers now. Wowee Zowee would be the first record released under the new arrangement. The Warners people were psyched. They were ready to get the publicity machine rolling and make the band stars. The Pavement guys were psyched. They knew they'd made a good record and were ready to tour. In a wild turnaround they'd been booked to play Lollapalooza. It was by far the best lineup in the festival's short history. The Jesus Lizard, Beck and Hole were on the bill. Sonic Youth was the headline act. Stephen picked Rattled by the Rush for the first single. It had hypnotic stuttering guitars and a staccato vocal pattern tough to get out of your head. It had a monster post-chorus riff. It had a catchy chant and killer guitar solo at the end. The time was still right for this kind of number. Rattled by the Rush was going to be big.

Summer 2007. I came out of the subway in Brooklyn wearing a suit and tie. I crossed over to the shady side of the street. I stopped at the deli and bought a six-pack of Blue Point. When I got home I put one in the freezer and the rest in the fridge. I changed out of my work clothes and returned to the kitchen. I cleared off the table and arranged my notebook and gear. At Radio Shack I'd purchased a small digital recorder, a cellphone earpiece and an adaptor that facilitated the recording of conversations. In a few minutes I was going to call Bob Nastanovich, Pavement's second drummer and utility man. I'd gotten his number from our mutual friend Sam. Bob and I had traded e-mails and established a time. Seeing his name in my inbox gave me a jolt.

I'd spent the day at work poring over my questions, feeling more confused than ever. The magic of Wowee Zowee seemed lost to me now. No matter how many times I played it the songs were just songs — great songs but still. I was starting to force shit. I was losing the thread.

I took the beer from the freezer and downed half for courage. I punched in Bob's number and hesitated before pressing send. I closed the phone and waited exactly three minutes. I dialed the number again and listened to it ring. The voice mail clicked on. I left a rambling message and sat there feeling relieved. I took some deep breaths and finished the beer. A few minutes later my girlfriend Karla arrived. We made tacos for dinner and drank the beer. I kept looking at my phone thinking it would ring but it didn't. In the morning I got up and checked it first thing. There were no new messages and no missed calls. I stood in the living room in my underwear. Months passed. A year.

Gerard Cosloy wrote the fanzine Conflict. For a time in the 80s he ran Homestead Records. Cosloy was college pals with J Mascis and Homestead put out the first Dinosaur LP. When Scott Kannberg was deciding where to send Slay Tracks for review, Conflict was high on the list. It turned out to be a good move. Cosloy said nice things about the record and became one of the earliest Pavement champions.

In 1990 Cosloy teamed up with Chris Lombardi to run Matador Records. The label was in its infancy when the two signed Pavement and released Slanted and Enchanted. Matador and a small handful of other labels defined indie in the 90s. For a few years mid-decade Pavement and Guided by Voices were Matador's flagship acts and all rock remotely classifiable as indie seemed descended from those two bands. I was scared to try to contact the Matador honchos. They were tastemakers who'd carved out their own little piece of rock history. In the face of this I ignored my own achievements and reverted to an old view of myself as a midwestern rube. I thought of when I first moved to New York and would go to this East Village record store, Kim's. I tried talking shop with the studs who worked there. They answered in single syllables and wouldn't meet my gaze. If that's how the record store guys treated me then what about the guys who actually put out the records?

I did some preliminary Internet research. To my surprise Gerard Cosloy had a MySpace page. I thought it over for a minute then composed a message. I told him about the book and said it would benefit from his insight. I came on heavy with my supposed credentials and ended up writing way too much. Cosloy wrote back saying if I had any specific questions fire away. Otherwise, he wrote, I prefer to keep my insight to myself. What did that mean — that he didn't want to talk to me but if I asked questions he would? I wrote back saying how do you want to do this. He responded with his e-mail address. I cut and pasted some questions and sent them along. No rush, I said, the more you can give me the better. Cosloy wrote back twenty-three minutes later. His answers were short and dickish. I read our exchange with a mix of humiliation and horror.

BC: From a fan's perspective, Pavement's rise during the Crooked Rain era — and the ascent of indie bands generally — was somewhat disorienting. There was a sense of being happy on one hand and quite protective and bitter on the other. What do you remember about that time? What strikes you about that era now looking back?

GC: I like thinking about what records sound like and how they're made. The ascent of indie bands generally is the least interesting thing I can possibly imagine thinking about. So I don't. I never considered Pavement an indie band.

BC: What were your first impressions of Wowee Zowee? What songs leapt out at you?

GC: I was pretty happy with the entire thing. I kept imagining how Rattled by the Rush was going to sound on KROQ. Talk about naive!

BC: Do you consider Wowee Zowee to be a challenging record?

GC: Compared to what? I think my short answer is no.

BC: What did you make of its relatively lukewarm reception?

GC: Everyone's entitled to their own screwy opinions.

BC: At what point did you realize a shift had begun in how the record was being perceived — from sprawling, confusing mess to diehard fan favorite?

GC: I've not realized that actually. I mean there are some people who loved it right from the get-go.

BC: Why do you think the record was so underrated initially? Why do you think it resonates so strongly now?

GC: These are impossible questions to answer. I didn't underrate the album initially. You're better off asking someone whose opinion changed over time rather than someone who loved it right away.

BC: Some people have interpreted Wowee Zowee as a kind of fuck-you record, Pavement taking a deliberate step back from potentially greater success. Do you think there's any truth to that?

GC: No. I mean it's really juvenile to assume Pavement had no other subject matter on their minds than their career trajectory. Just because they traded in humor doesn't mean their albums were meant to be a running commentary on being in a semi-popular band.

The least interesting thing he could imagine thinking about? Everyone's entitled to their own screwy opinions? Impossible questions/juvenile assumptions? The archetypal indie band not actually an indie band? I stewed and fretted, feeling like a big fucking geek. My worst fears had been realized — black waves of record store anxiety redux. Karla and I watched a couple episodes of Deadwood then went to bed.

In the morning I wrote Cosloy back. His reply came in less than an hour.

BC: Your point is well taken — on paper maybe the ascent of indie bands generally isn't the most scintillating topic. But there's no question Matador brought a new kind of music to a much broader audience.

GC: I'm sorry. I hardly think there's no question. We were somewhat successful in helping a handful of bands scale new commercial heights. But our interest was in those specific bands. We've never been advocates for a new kind of music.

BC: I was just looking for a line or two about what it was like seeing artists you championed — whose records didn't sound like what had previously been popular — reach greater heights than perhaps even they had imagined.

GC: You'll just have to keep hoping then.

BC: If not indie what kind of band do you consider Pavement to be?

GC: They're a rock and roll band. I don't believe indie is actually a musical genre.

BC: Do you consider Wowee Zowee challenging compared to Pavement's previous two records?

GC: No. I think the songs are fantastic. The entire notion of challenging strikes me as bogus. I mean if you found yourself challenged, fair enough, but that's your take, not mine. Any artist worth his or her salt is just trying to write what they like — the audience's anxieties shouldn't ever enter the picture.

BC: I don't doubt that you and many others loved Wowee Zowee immediately. But it seems clear there was also great resistance to it at the time. Surely you've thought about that, or you did then. Why do you think certain listeners found it inaccessible?

GC: I don't know. I mean I have my suspicions (i.e. they were morons), but unless I actually ask them I'll never know for sure. And again, you're asking me to put myself into the tiny head of someone else. If you're interested in why someone else didn't dig Wowee Zowee, it seems you oughta be identifying those persons. Or better yet, examining your own feelings about the album rather than expecting me to confirm your hypothesis. And no, I didn't surely think about it at the time. There's a million and one reasons why a record or a band captures the public's imagination. Some of those reasons are entirely nonmusical.

I stewed and fretted. I took a walk. I eked out minimal perspective. I wrote Cosloy back.

I wrote: When you say you don't believe indie is actually a musical genre, are you suggesting the word should only be used to literally describe a certain type of non-major record label? Or that words like indie or alternative or whatever have no value at all? I ask because Matador is more closely aligned with the word indie than probably any other label except Merge.

I wrote: Also it strikes me as somewhat disingenuous to say you released records — especially a highly anticipated follow-up by one of your label's biggest bands — without giving a thought to their reception, whether positive, negative or indifferent. So let me put it another way: having loved Wowee Zowee from the get-go, were you at any time confused or disappointed by its relatively lukewarm reception?

I clicked send and waited. He didn't respond.

The interaction left me shaken. It spoke to a series of buried doubts. Maybe Gerard Cosloy was right. Maybe my questions were bullshit. Maybe my macro theories were bunk. Was Wowee Zowee so underrated at first? Was it such a critical and commercial dud? Do people really love it so much now? I searched the Internet for reviews. Everything I found referenced the 2006 reissue. Those items all followed a similar plotline and seemed to confirm my thinking: this was a strange record, no one got it at first, we all sat with it for a while, we all love it now. But where were those old bad reviews? The only original one I found was from Rolling Stone. It begins: What does a defiantly anti-corporate rock band do when it starts getting too much attention? It retreats. Slanted and Enchanted is then described as something of a masterpiece. Crooked Rain is said to have confirmed Pavement's buzz-band status. Wowee Zowee is introduced as a doggedly experimental album with

disappointing results. Pavement is accused of not understanding their own songwriting impulses — they weren't
sure whether they were mocking something or imitating
it. Rattled by the Rush, Grounded, Kennel District and
Father to a Sister of Thought are singled out for praise.
Brinx Job, Serpentine Pad, Best Friend's Arm etc. are
dismissed as half-baked, gratuitous, whiny, tossed-off,
second-rate Sonic Youth, unfinished rehearsals, empty
experimentation. The last line: Maybe this album is a
radical message to the corporate-rock ogre — or maybe
Pavement are simply afraid to succeed.

There it is. The old self-sabotage bit. But was Rolling
Stone really anyone's barometer of quality? What about
the dude who wrote the review? Did he have some glo-
rious resume of achievement to coast on? Given ten
lifetimes could he conjure a melody to rival even the
laziest effort of Stephen Malkmus? I haven't done any
digging. I can't say for sure. One lesson was clear: moth-
erfuck Rolling Stone.

I contemplated shitcanning the whole project. I had
a single original review and no sales figures. I still hadn't
talked to anyone in the band. I half thought rock writing
itself was a fucking scam. I'd finally finished my novel
but it had big problems and needed a slash-and-burn
rewrite that would take many months. I'd blown through
my bankroll and needed a job. A little voice said no. A
little voice said wait. I kept thinking of this thing that
happened shortly after I moved to the city. It was a small
moment but for some reason it stuck with me. I was
walking around exploring with my headphones on — this
would have been October of 98. A Wowee Zowee track

called AT&T was playing. There's a line in it that goes *spritzer on ice in New York City, isn't it a pity you never had anything to mix with that?* and right at that line I turned a corner and was on Park Avenue and saw the MetLife building in the distance. It must have been midday. There were people rushing around. It was overcast. I paused on the sidewalk and looked around as if aware for the first time of where in the universe I was. Suddenly some of the terror of moving here fell away. I felt a surge of pure freedom. I'd been here what, maybe two or three weeks. I had no history in New York. My life was unwritten. All that I would do and see and be here lay ahead. The air felt alive. It hummed and crackled with possibility. Stephen Malkmus urged me forward — *one two three GO!* — in a long joyous shout. A moment later I reentered the human flow. We walked the plank in the dark.

I met Chris Lombardi at the Matador offices on Hudson Street. I sat waiting by the front desk and checked out the scene. It was similar to the Virgin Records office I'd temped in. There were band posters everywhere and loud music played — except the posters were of bands I liked and the music was good. Lombardi appeared. We went into his office. He was in the middle of switching spaces and everything was in disarray. He said he'd been listening to Wowee Zowee right before I showed up. He had the reissue booklet in his hands and flipped through it a moment.

— By the time of Wowee Zowee, he said, — Pavement had money to spend and ideas to burn. And so they went and tried some stuff. I think they stepped back from things a little bit. There was an ambivalence. They didn't necessarily want to go for the brass ring. There's no doubt they were working hard. They were a hard-working band. They were touring all the time. People who liked them might have been frustrated. I think a lot of people thought, this is some of the best songwriting out there. Pavement was fresh-sounding and adventuresome. There was always just that feeling that if Steve would have changed that lyric around a little bit . . . He would always throw that wrench into the song that would be something goofy, an in-joke for him or somebody else in the band or a slag on something that ultimately was kind of the curveball that kept them from knocking it out of the park. There was a sense that these guys should be the biggest band in the world. Why are the Smashing Pumpkins the biggest band in the world right now? This is retarded. I think that was probably part of people's frustration with Pavement. They were like, these guys are so good. They're obviously super smart and super talented. They can fucking play circles and write circles around any of these other idiot bands. Stone Temple Pilots or some bullshit. Why can't Pavement be the most popular band in the world?

Funny he should mention those two bands. Maybe it was an intentional or unconscious allusion to Range Life — in which STP also takes a hit: *Stone Temple Pilots, they're elegant bachelors, they're foxy to me, are they foxy to you? I will agree, they deserve absolutely nothing, nothing more than me.* I smiled when Lombardi said this. I didn't — couldn't — tell him I love both bands.

Smashing Pumpkins are one of my all-time faves. I got into them early and stayed with them unequivocally through Adore. Fandom became a trickier proposition after that. Billy Corgan starting pulling all kinds of deranged shit. He made a mostly terrible record — MACHINA/The Machines of God — then blamed everyone but himself when it didn't sell. He announced the Pumpkins were disbanding because they couldn't compete with the Britneys of the world. He formed a decent power pop group, Zwan. He ditched the black gowns in favor of earth-tone indie garb. He broke up Zwan and trashed all the members — minus drummer and musical soul mate Jimmy Chamberlin — to anyone who would take notes. He published a book of terrible poems — blurbed by JT LeRoy, a starfucking figment of some addled starfucker's imagination.

Corgan started a blog. He wrote new-age posts about forgiveness, healing and god. Other posts oozed Nixonian paranoia and trashed old friends, bandmates, engineers — this time including Jimmy Chamberlin, whose 90s drug fuckups he chronicled at length. He said his remarks about the Britneys of the world had been misconstrued and blamed the Pumpkins' dissolution on James Iha — a little like suggesting Porl Thompson could break up the Cure. He made an underrated electropop record. He did that record no favors by taking out newspaper ads the day it came out announcing his intention to re-form Smashing Pumpkins. The new band — Corgan, Chamberlin, three charisma-free hired hands — hit the scene two years later. For some reason Corgan dressed everyone in flowing white robes with spacesuit collars.

A new record came out, the mediocre-to-bad Zeitgeist. It failed to zoom Corgan back to his mid-90s peak. He launched an epic bitchfest, contradicting himself and/or insulting fans at every turn. He said even though Smashing Pumpkins had gotten back together and made a new record what you were seeing was not a reunion. He said they weren't going to be like other bands that re-form and just play the old hits. Those bands lacked integrity, they were slaves to their audiences' demands. Corgan insisted he wasn't anyone's puppet. He could not be constrained or told what to do. He wondered why people didn't love the Zeitgeist tune Bleeding the Orchid. That's a great song, he said, it could have been on Siamese Dream. He wondered why people just stood there blinking when he played formless acoustic tunes written hours earlier at his hotel. He said he wasn't going to release albums anymore — no one listens to them so why bother. What he'd do instead was release two or three songs at a time digitally over a period of years. He broke down the cultural moment in the manner of a sophomore on a hit of reefer — these days everyone's being spoonfed, everything's rigged to give people exactly what they want, fuck that.

I caught the new Pumpkins on their twentieth-anniversary tour. I'd never seen Corgan live. A nostalgic/curious muscle flexed. I dropped $132 for two nights at the United Palace Theater. Bad move. The stage was cluttered with session players — horns, strings, keyboards etc. Corgan wore a form-fitting dress. Long stretches of both sets were given over to tuneless metal riffing and ponderous noise-blip jams. A Pink Floyd cover stretched to thirty minutes. A Simon and Garfunkel cover was unrecognizable sludge. None of the hired hands moved, smiled or spoke. Corgan veered between hostile silence and expressions of gratitude and love. At the end of the first night he rapped a line of passive-aggressive bile while the band stood behind him playing kazoos. He responded to negative comments from the crowd that — at least that night — didn't appear to have been made. He mocked those who wanted to hear their favorite songs and said he'd see us in hell. The next night he let a moron vent spleen on stage then ran a middle-school-level sodomy riff when the guy sat down. The whole experience was a depressing mess. Any goodwill I still had for the man expired with a pop.

I mulled over those concerts for days afterward. One thought recurred: Billy Corgan as the anti-Stephen Malkmus. Maybe I had them on the brain together because of Range Life. In my head there were parallels that transcended their association via that song. Both are favorites of mine going back to my late teens. Both led revered and influential bands. Both are guitar virtuosos with signature styles. Both started solo careers at around the same time. But Corgan has spent the years since then adrift. Malkmus has yet to make a bad/false/wrong move. Corgan seems constantly ill at ease. Malkmus seems to exist in a state of permanent sangfroid. Corgan is stuck in a weird cycle of announcing/repudiating increasingly baroque schemes to challenge his audience and bring his music to new markets. Malkmus releases great records every other year with no fanfare — twenty-one years in he's never made a bad or even a weak one. Malkmus doesn't make sweeping statements about where rock is headed or talk about all the mind-blowing shit he's gonna do — he just fucking does it. If some portion of his audience didn't follow him where he wanted to go I doubt he'd blame a pleasure-centric culture bent on instant gratification or give interviews declaring a lack of faith in his audience. No — he'd tour for the record and make another one, tour for that record, make another one etc.

Summer 2008. Karla and I were traveling to France. We arrived at JFK around four p.m. and breezed through security with an hour to kill before our flight. We stopped at a restaurant called Soho Bistro. Karla ordered a burger. I ordered a wine. I popped a Xanax. I'd copped the tablets from a friend. I used to have my own prescription but my health insurance ran out and I can't board a plane sober. Every time I get on an airplane I think I'm going to die.

Our seats were in the last row of the middle section and didn't recline. I squeezed in and sat there trying to hold it together. A guy across the row from me was filing his nails. The noise scorched my nerves. I leveled a hate stare. The guy didn't notice. I wanted to slap the nail file away, shake him, scream. He filed only the left thumbnail. He would file for a few seconds then run his left index finger along the thumbnail, discover some imperfection, begin filing again. Look at that fucking guy, I said to Karla, what the fuck is he doing, who files their nails on an airplane, what the fuck is that about? My heart was jackhammering. I dripped cold sweat. Karla smiled. She touched my arm. She told me it was okay.

The man put his nail file away. We pulled back from the gate. The plane taxied and took off. The person in front of me reclined. Their seat pressed into my knees. Everything closed in on me. I imagined an explosion, steel shredding me, my body in flames. How could I get through six more hours of this shit? I discussed the matter with Karla. I hailed a flight attendant and asked if there was any way I could move. You're in luck, she said, there's an exit row seat just a few rows back. She asked if I was willing and able to assist in the event of an emergency. I said yes.

I stretched out in my new seat and popped another tablet. They came around with the beverage cart. I ordered a wine — free on international flights. I ordered another with dinner. I popped a tablet. It grew dark at the window. They cut the overhead lights. The movie came on. Evan Almighty. I put in my earbuds and scrolled through my iPod. Nothing leapt out at me. The curse of the mp3 era — thousands of hours of music at your fingertips and you never want to hear any of it, nothing ever leaps out you. The blue bar rolled over Wowee Zowee. I hesitated, rolled it back, pressed play. I sank down in my seat and closed my eyes. The first note of the first song is a lonesome plucked E string. Sad tinkling piano. Faint exhalation of disgust or defeat. It jumps to A. Malkmus sings *there is no . . . castration fear* — Something clicked into place then. The thick mists cleared. I thought, holy shit, this is fucking it! I heard Wowee Zowee as I'd first heard it a thousand years ago, before I moved to the city, before all my shit jobs, before a plane blew up my office, before these endless fucking wars. The record held me. The magic was there. All current music suddenly withered in comparison. Who takes chances like this these days? Who has this kind of fun?

When it was over I went to see Karla. We watched the end of Evan Almighty with no sound. I returned to my seat and popped a tablet. I phased in and out of consciousness. Now and then I looked around at the sleeping people. I wanted to keep everyone safe, even the nail file guy. Please let us land, I thought, please just let me get down from here. I didn't know who or what I was addressing. A bright orange line formed on the black horizon. I glanced at my watch. Time was compressed up here. Time was fucked up. It was only midnight. It was already dawn.

Bob Nastanovich joined Pavement in a desperation move and became a band linchpin and secret weapon. He joined initially to prop up Gary Young. Gary was so out of it at times he wouldn't know what song they were playing. As Pavement began touring more Stephen's voice would go from nightly abuse. Bob took on the more abrasive vocal parts live. He yelled I'M TRYIN! on Conduit for Sale. He yelled DEBRIS SLIDE! on Debris Slide. He yelled WALK! WITH YOUR CREDIT CARD IN THE AIR! on Unfair. He played all kinds of percussion — maracas, hi-hat, tambourine, cowbell. Around the time of Wowee Zowee he bought a Moog. He didn't know how to play keyboard per se but he knew how to make interesting noises on a synthesizer. He had free rein to do whatever he wanted. Stephen wouldn't even pay attention. Sometimes two months into a tour he'd say to Bob, I don't know what you're doing over there but it must be pretty good because people say you're doing a good job.

Bob was a key member of Pavement from early on but Wowee Zowee is the first full-length he was in the studio for. Prior to that his studio input was minimal. He was there for the Watery, Domestic sessions — the last to feature Gary on drums. That was Bob's first time in California. He wrote a travelogue chronicling his first forty-eight hours in the state. Stephen dug it. Bob recorded it as a spoken word bit. They stuck it at the end of Sue Me Jack, one of a string of extraordinary early b-sides. Wowee Zowee was different. They'd played many of the songs live on various Crooked Rain tours. Bob had parts to play and therefore tracks to lay down. On Wowee Zowee he sings or plays on almost every song. That's him screaming in the background on Serpentine Pad, a track that comes close to approximating the Bob phenomenon live. Bob's energy was crucial to the Pavement concert experience. He always looked like he was having a blast. That sounds like a small thing but after years on the road playing all the same songs most people start to go through the motions at least a little bit. Bob never did.

— The whole thing was incredibly exciting for me, he told me. — I'd started to go see bands when I was twelve years old and twelve years later to be in the kind of band I would have loved was very exciting for me.

I asked him to take me through the Crooked Rain period.

— I think the interesting thing about Crooked Rain that seems to have made a lot of Pavement fans uncomfortable was that it wasn't their precious little band anymore. This band that they'd followed for a few years — some of them even before Slanted and

Enchanted — had always been the fans' band. It's not like it was a secret or anything like that because there was always people there. But it was the definition of a cult following. And just all at once — really sort of based on not only what we were doing but also most significantly the effect of Nirvana on the music industry — all of a sudden all these people, mostly young people, were turning their attention to underground acts. What was being put in their face at the time was bands like Pavement. All of a sudden we were playing two or three times as many shows during Crooked Rain and there were a lot more people coming out and there was more sustained interest. We'd get a lot of crowds where half the people knew the band really well and really liked the band and the other half would just be trying to figure out if they liked that kind of music. So it was pretty interesting from that standpoint because people were trying out Pavement to see if they liked it. Things sort of happened fast at that time but they didn't feel like they were happening too fast. During the rise and leveling off of Pavement our fame never reached a level where it made any of us uncomfortable. We'd worked very hard and done just about everything on our own, up to a certain point. We were actually able to hire people to help us — and still feel like it was financially prudent. Pavement, more than a lot of other bands from the same era, were very shrewd. We wanted to work hard and we wanted to make money. We never canceled a show. And a lot of that was getting to places under very adverse circumstances.

— Did you ever get burned out touring?

— Oh yeah. Terrible. I drank a lot. The food

sometimes was good and sometimes was crap. You get sick and then you still have to go on. I mean you can't just say I'm sick. I'm not complaining. I'm not saying the whole thing wasn't incredibly fun and we didn't have a blast. It was a classic case of too much fun. It got to the point toward the end of the year, a lot of those years, where I would hide in the bus or the van, just to put myself in the isolation tank because I didn't want to talk to people. And then when I did have to talk to people I wanted to make sure that I was going to present myself as a nice person. It's just part of caring. Caring about those people that came and saw the band. They were incredibly important to us.

— That's one of the paradoxes of the band. There was this lazy tag that followed Pavement around, that you guys were slackers and you didn't care.

— Malkmus was the focal point of the band, deservedly so. He wrote most of the songs. And that's sort of the way he carries himself, more than anybody else. Plus from a fashion standpoint we pretty much dressed the same way in Pavement as we all did when we were fifteen years old. That was part of the whole movement, the start of indie rock: rock is not about dressing up, it's about wearing whatever you're comfortable in. We all wanted to look good but we all wanted to present ourselves exactly as we were. Stephen's body language and the way he's pretty nonchalant about his clothing — a lot of the things he wore on stage in Pavement he borrowed from me. He would have lost his clothes. I think that whole slacker, lazy tag really comes from him and how he presents himself and this whole sort of I don't really care, it doesn't really matter thing. If I had a dollar for every single time he said, it doesn't matter, I wouldn't have to work.

Bob laughed. — So that's where that whole thing comes from. It's not like Stephen did not work. He's obsessively working on his songs. But it's the way he carried himself — and still carries himself to this day.

— It's funny you say that about clothes. That's one of the things I miss about that era. With a lot of indie bands now it's more of a dress-up thing, with tight western shirts and things like that.

— That kind of thing is coming back, actual rock and roll fashion. But basically from the mid-80s through the 90s, all the Sub Pop bands, the whole grunge thing, it was T-shirts and corduroys or T-shirts and jeans or maybe a golf shirt. Whatever you wore — whatever you'd wear anyways on your days off — that's what people wore. The Strokes were pretty high fashion. Even Franz Ferdinand and bands like that. There's a lot of beards now in indie rock. A lot of the cool bands are these guys with beards. I don't know what it is. West always had a huge beard. But he's an insane Civil War buff so that's where that comes from. And Berman, David Berman often has a beard. I think they think it makes them look like historic figures or something. Which I guess both of them are in their own way.

In their Jersey City/Hoboken days Berman, Malkmus and Nastanovich formed a living-room group called the Silver Jews. The Jews evolved from making primitive home recordings to become a full-fledged studio band. Membership was fluid. David Berman was the only constant. For a while in the 90s three-fifths of Pavement — Malkmus, Bob and Steve West — was in the band. The Jews recorded their Starlite Walker LP at Easley Recording in Memphis. In 94 they returned to do another full-length. Berman flaked and quit the scene. Malkmus, Nastanovich and West used the time to record Pavement songs instead. The result was the Pacific Trim EP. Everyone dug the Easley vibe. It made sense to go back there to do Wowee Zowee.

— We were very comfortable at Easley, said Bob. — Everybody knew what to expect. Memphis was really cool because we're all barbecue enthusiasts. I think during the entire process at most times I had sauce crusted on my face. I gained like twenty pounds. All we did was eat barbecue and drink beer. We went out a lot. It was fun. It was very easy to make Wowee Zowee because I think most of us knew what we were doing. The problem was, we kept recording all these songs. We got two-thirds of the way through the process and we were trying to figure out, should we make this album conventional length or should we leave it all on there? Should we save some songs for an EP or what? In the end we decided everything we had was album-worthy so it all came out at once. We didn't really put any thought into the fact that it was complicated, not as easy to swallow as Crooked Rain. That was Pavement. We had all those songs, we were happy with all those songs and happy with the way they were recorded. We thought they were all good and wanted to put them all out.

— At that time there was a lot of talk about Pavement fielding big-money offers from major labels. Was that something the band took seriously? Was there ever a moment where you were truly wondering what do to next?

— First of all, there were never any feelings like, no we don't want to be successful. We wanted to be as successful as possible within the confines of our collective taste. We weren't going to do anything really, really lame or embarrassing to be successful. That was a misconception about Pavement. I think people always sort of thought, oh they made an album like Wowee Zowee intentionally to stay on the ground or to push back certain elements of the music industry. But in truth, nobody contacted us at all during that period with any ridiculous offers.

— Really? There were never any concrete offers from the major labels?

— I think maybe after Slanted there were, before Crooked Rain. But I don't even know because I would not have been privy to that. You'd have to ask Scott. Or even Gary. Gary was drunk so he would get approached. There's some story he'll tell you about how before he played a show in Hoboken one time he was at Columbia Records or something and they got him all drunk and they offered him a million dollars. He showed up late for the show. At this point I don't really know if that's true. But I guess they shipped him over in a limo so he actually was in there. Who knows. It could have been part delirium tremens or something. It might have been entirely unreal. No, we were very happy with the situation at Matador. We knew all the people there and they'd sort of started at the same time we did. We had an unusually good deal with them and we were making plenty off the records and on tour. Again, we wanted to be successful. But we also felt like we were. So there wasn't this dissatisfaction. One great thing about Pavement, from day one, there was always people at the shows, there was always a huge amount of interest in the band. Around the band there was always this feeling — not that we couldn't do anything wrong, because we made mistakes all the time. A lot of them had to do with the fact that we disdained practicing. There was always a feeling — not like a confident swagger — but there was always a feeling that we were important.

— I would have thought there would have been all kinds of offers. Plenty of lesser bands were getting huge deals then.

— In all honesty you would have found out before I would have. That's Kannberg's territory. It would have been him and Malkmus. Definitely Kannberg. He would have been more interested in that aspect of the situation, so he could actually define what was going on. From my standpoint it was like, okay what are we doing in the next six months.

Scott Kannberg — aka Spiral Stairs, aka Spiral. Kannberg co-founded Pavement and wrote at least one of the band's best songs, Wowee Zowee's Kennel District. He wrote a few others almost as good that wound up as b-sides or compilation tracks. Outtake status can be an unpromising sign but Pavement's non-album tracks are better than most bands' best shit. There's a Wowee-era Kannberg tune called Painted Soldiers that easily could have been on that record or even, with cleaner production, on Brighten the Corners — it might have fit better than his tune Passat Dream. Instead it landed on the Brain Candy soundtrack. Kannberg favors woo-hoo/bop-bop vocal patterns and Painted Soldiers has a catchy woo-ooh hook. It also features one of the best Pavement videos: Spiral fires everyone in the band and remakes Pavement with himself as the leader and members of Veruca Salt following his direction. The characterizations are priceless. Mark Ibold plays a greasy bully/pimp, Steve West plays a creepy suburban swinger/pedophile, Malkmus plays a fast-driving hotshot cruising in a red sports car with a babe at his side. Only Bob hews more or less close to the truth, playing a dapper horse racing aficionado who gets canned at the track. I didn't see the Painted Soldiers video till the Slow Century DVD came out in late 2002. The notion of Kannberg firing Malkmus struck me as darkly humorous in light of the band's actual songwriting dynamic and then-recent breakup.

Post-Pavement, Kannberg released two albums under the name Preston School of Industry and one as Spiral Stairs. His solo work generally is underrated. The first Preston School record in particular got a raw deal. Bad timing maybe — it came out six months after Malkmus's solo debut and two weeks before 9/11. But some of Kannberg's best songs — Whalebones, Falling Away, Encyclopedic Knowledge of — are on that. Five years passed between the next Preston LP and The Real Feel — the first album credited to Spiral Stairs. The Real Feel is Kannberg's most personal, cohesive record. It has some heavy divorce tunes and an autumnal gestalt. His solo singing is fuller and stronger across the board.

Kannberg's Pavement album tracks range in quality from the sublime — Kennel District, Date with IKEA — to the arguably swappable — Hit the Plane Down, Passat Dream. It's hard to be objective about this since I essentially like all Pavement album tracks at this point and can't imagine the records with different running orders. But there was a time when I left Western Homes off every tape I made of Wowee Zowee. It's an easy edit, the last song on the record. For a good five or six years I thought it should have been cut. I wasn't alone — Kannberg himself told me he wanted to give it the ax. But not because he didn't like it. He favored a shorter running order for the record. He also wanted to cut Brinx Job, Serpentine Pad, Extradition, Best Friend's Arm and Flux = Rad. Those songs sounded like b-sides to him. Most of them were done in New York with only Malkmus, Ibold and West. They didn't fit with the vibe of the other tunes.

— Steve and me, we really bickered on that. He wanted certain songs on there that I just didn't want. I wanted it to be more the songs we played as a band at Easley's. Steve wanted to bring it back to the way he thought Pavement should be — a little more loose. I was thinking, this is our Reckoning or this is our Lifes Rich Pageant. I thought of it in terms of other bands or classic rock records. And it was kinda funny because our next record, Brighten the Corners, ended up being more of a classic, traditional kind of record.

— Cutting Western Homes seems like a modest move, I said. — You don't usually hear about people in bands wanting to cut their own contributions.

— No. But I think now it fits well in the context of the record. Because it is very different from some of the other songs. It's a pretty good last song.

— That's actually how I came to appreciate it. Western Homes really grew on me. I didn't like it for the longest time.

— Yeah. That one is kinda like, whoa what's this?

— So what are your songs on Wowee Zowee about? Kennel District and Western Homes sound like pretty specific titles.

— Kennel District I wrote when we were doing

Crooked Rain. We recorded it then and it just didn't sound good. Kennel District is basically just the title. The song has a completely different theme. You know how when you're walking around New York it has all the different districts, the diamond district, the fashion district. I envisioned having a kennel district, where they kept all the dogs in New York.

He laughed. — I used to do that a lot. I used to have titles different from what the song had anything to do with. Date with IKEA is like that as well — the title has nothing to do with the song. Western Homes, on the other hand, does. It's based on suburbia and where I grew up and how everything was changing into very crappy brand-new suburbs. Western homes, locked forever — I can't even remember the lyrics. But look at it now. The area outside of Stockton I was talking about is the foreclosure capital of America, the ghetto of the future.

— Friends of mine from California don't say many good things about Stockton.

— Well there's cool little areas of it, the older areas. In the 70s and 80s there was a lot of money there but it was all in agriculture and they always fought against professional jobs going there. So everything moved to Sacramento, everything went to the Bay Area. Stockton kinda got left behind. Then in the late 90s all these suburbs for the Bay Area, for Silicon Valley, started sprouting up around Stockton. There was just no stopping it. Western Homes is based on an old Roxy Music song — In Every Dream Home a Heartache, on either their first or second record. It's based on that. I really like the sound of it, I like the way it turned out. It's still one of my favorite songs that I've ever done. It's pretty weird. I don't think any of my other songs sounded that weird.

— What about Kennel District? That sounds to me with that one refrain — why didn't I ask? — like a love song.

— Yeah it kind of is. I think when I wrote it I was broken up with my girlfriend, soon to be wife. It was a love song for her. I think I broke up with her because I was in the band and I was just never around and I think she needed me to be there more than I was. A lot of the lyrics had to do with her, especially that line. I can't believe she's married to rope — that line juxtaposes my girlfriend against this woman who'd been married to a guy I met in New York. The woman told me the guy always beat her. So married to rope is being tied down. Those couple lines in there are juxtaposed against the lines about my girlfriend. I think she wanted more of a relationship with me and I didn't want it. At the same time I'm meeting this woman who loves this guy who's beating her, and who's married to her. So it's like this weird . . .

He paused. He laughed. — I don't know what I was thinking, dude. It's nonsense almost. It wasn't that well thought out.

— What's that odd high-pitched noise on the melody? It sounds like some kind of guitar effect but I can't nail it down.

— That's a weird keyboard. Fuck, what was it? I'd never seen it before. It was a weird kind of phase-shifting Moog. But it wasn't a Moog, it was something else. I wish I still had that. I found it at a garage sale. One of our guitar techs was really into weird electronic music before anybody ever was and he snapped it up from me. It's on Western Homes as well — the fuzzy noise sound on that. When we'd play Kennel District live Malkmus would recreate that part on his guitar, that melody.

— Yeah but it never sounded the same.

— No. I think Matador wanted to try to do Kennel District as a single but they wanted to rerecord it. I kind of wanted to because it's pretty noisy.

— It's noisy but I can see that impulse, someone looking at Wowee Zowee and thinking, okay what's the single?

— Yeah what'd we put out? Rattled by the Rush. Oh god.

Kannberg laughed. — Rattled was good. It's just . . . funny. It was a pretty weird song for that time period to put out as a single.

I backtracked to Crooked Rain. Kannberg said they never expected to get that big. It was a combination of touring hard on their own and going out with Sonic Youth — that was a lucky break. In their minds the second record was a continuation of what they'd already been doing. The only difference was Gary Young wasn't around. With Steve West on drums the band felt more stable, for Malkmus especially.

— But it was such a short little period, he said. — Cut Your Hair came out and got played on a few modern rock stations and then all of sudden it disappears and then it's Bush. And then the real major-label bands took over. So that was basically it for us. They tried with some other songs, Range Life or whatever, but we couldn't compete against Weezer and Bush and all those what I like to call manager-driven bands.

— I was nineteen or twenty then and I was naive. I assumed any band that was on MTV had made it, they were rolling in dough.

— You know what we were doing? Right when that song came out we were doing a Canadian tour, basically driving nine hours every day and Bob would, instead of putting the money in the bank Bob would put all the money in the trunk. We'd make a couple thousand dollars a show — if that. That was a big show. There were little perks that came with being on MTV. We got to play on 120 Minutes and famous people came to our shows for a little bit and we got to be on Jay Leno.

— That must have been a little weird, being on Jay Leno.

— Oh it was surreal. But it just seemed kind of funny to us. Like this is what the Replacements would have done. I always thought of things in terms of them. It was like, right now we're like the Replacements when they were on Saturday Night Live. Let's act like them.

I asked if any major labels were after Pavement. Kannberg said no, that was all hype. The band kind of played that stuff up in the press. Matador kept major-label people away from them. But there was a meeting in LA once. They flew there to pitch Wowee Zowee to Warner Brothers. Weird shit happened. Kannberg asked if I'd heard about it.

— Vaguely. What was that like?

— Danny Goldberg had just become president of Warners and we were going to do Lollapalooza and everything so we wanted to have this meeting with him. Gerard and Chris were there and Steve and I were there. We had this meeting with Danny Goldberg and some other vice president or something. Gerard's giving this speech about Pavement, asking what Warners was going to do for us and how they were going to promote us, and the whole time Danny Goldberg is on the phone talking to somebody. And it's kind of uneasy because it's like he's not listening. Finally Gerard gets mad and says hey dude, obviously you don't want us here, what the fuck? Danny Goldberg says ah this record's shit, or something like that. He looked at the other Warners people and said what do you guys wanna do? I don't think we can do anything with this record. It was like, great. Thanks. Oh man, Gerard was so mad. I think the minute that happened he was on the phone with his lawyer. The weird thing about Warners, there were some really cool people that worked there and loved our record and tried really hard. At that time I started becoming more active in making sure that I would contact these people and talk to them about what we were doing. And they were really nice and they tried hard but when the president of the label says Whatever, it's a bad sign.

He laughed. — I don't blame him really. If I would have heard Wowee Zowee after Crooked Rain I would have been the same way.

— Some people think it was a deliberate fuck-you.

— Not at all, man. Not at all. That's the weird thing about it. I think the reason why is it starts with We Dance. Steve definitely wanted We Dance first. That's a pretty dark song coming after Cut Your Hair.

— It's interesting that some people think that about Pavement. They didn't want to be big, they thought they were too big.

— Yeah well. You can promote that myth if you want.

Danny Goldberg came up in times of rock purity and excess. He was vice president of Led Zeppelin's Swan Song Records in the 70s. In the 80s he started a management company, Gold Mountain. He kept a toe in the underground. Sonic Youth and Nirvana became clients. Goldberg was tight with Kurt Cobain. He was present at an ill-fated intervention late in Cobain's life. It was weird calling Goldberg for this reason. I was a huge Nirvana fan. Nevermind hit when I was seventeen and I went deep with it. I believed Kurt's drug-use denials. I believed the official statement — issued by Gold Mountain — that said Kurt slipped into a coma accidentally after popping a few chilling tablets with a splash of champagne. Goldberg's assistant put me on hold. A moment later he came on the line.

— Yeah, he said. — Go.

— All right. Well. When did you first hear of Pavement?

— I know I had heard of them before Wowee Zowee.

I had heard Slanted and Enchanted when it came out. I don't remember when. I mean I wasn't the first person to hear it. But there was enough critical acclaim for Slanted and Enchanted that it came to my attention at some point and I'd heard it. So by the time I spoke to Matador when Crooked Rain was going to come out I was familiar with Slanted and Enchanted.

— And how did the deal with Matador come about?

— I went to Atlantic Records from being a manager. My job there was to bring in new music and to try to modernize Atlantic's roster in the rock area. They had some big rock records. You know, Phil Collins and the great legacy with Led Zeppelin. Some very smart people there but with the burgeoning of indie rock they had underperformed a little bit. They had some acts, they had the Lemonheads, they had a few other things. But it wasn't happening. And I asked Kim Gordon and Thurston Moore what to do. I asked the artists I had worked with. Nirvana and Sonic Youth knew much more about music than I did. Especially Sonic Youth. They were so integral to exposing people as opening acts and just knowledgeable about all the indie labels. And they told me Matador was the best indie label and if there was any way I could be involved with them I would be lucky. You know, I did my homework. At that time Superchunk and Pavement were the two kind of marquee acts that Matador had. Gerard had his history as a critic and tastemaker and all that. I called Gerard — it was either Gerard or Chris Lombardi. I think I called Gerard and said are you interested in working with a major label? Do you need money? Do you need distribution? I guess they did. So we gave them a deal where if things didn't happen they could get the company back. They had complete control over who they signed and who they hired and how they operated. But there was some marketing help, distribution and some finance from Atlantic in return for half ownership and the distribution fees. With some months of discussion with them to reassure them that they could do things the way they wanted to do them. But it obviously worked out from their point of view enough to sign the deal. I was very proud of it. So that was the context in the Atlantic period. I then moved over to Warner Brothers. There was a corporate shakeup at Warner Music and I became the chairman of Warner Brothers. Gerard said, we were at Atlantic because of you and it's weird without you and could we put out the next Pavement record through Warners instead of Atlantic? And Val Azzoli — the chairman of Atlantic — didn't care. He said fine, you can have it.

— Was there any expectation that the follow-up to Crooked Rain would be an even bigger record and that Pavement would become a bigger band?

— Those expectations were dampened by Gerard and by Stephen Malkmus. Especially Stephen was really into downplaying any kind of expectations and not really wanting to be involved with some of the things that an artist would do. Certainly at Warner Brothers we had a lot of other artists. It wasn't the dynamic to pressure them into doing anything they didn't want to do. But Stephen was very clearly not going to play any of the games or do any of the things that might increase the odds of it happening. He was the one member of the band I spoke to. I didn't get to know the other guys at all. And Stephen just wasn't into it. He wanted to do what he wanted to do and keep the quality of life he had. He loved the intensity of the fans he had but didn't want to disrupt his inner rhythms and lifestyle. I really respected that. But you know, obviously when an artist isn't pushing what can a label do?

I told him I'd heard about a meeting with Matador and two of the Pavement guys. Gerard was pushing Wowee Zowee. You were checked out. You were on the phone or something, not listening. You said the record was shit and nothing could be done with it.

— That's absolutely not true, said Goldberg. — I would never have said anything like that. First of all I wouldn't have said that to Pavement and I certainly would never have said that about anything on Matador. I mean I had the highest respect for Chris and Gerard and I still do. And I really walked on eggs to try to be respectful of them. I thought they were special people who did things their own way. When I was at Warner Brothers I was thrust into a maelstrom of music business political chaos. All the senior executives were trying to figure out whether they wanted to leave the company or stay at the company. All these superstars — whether it was Madonna, Prince, Neil Young, Eric Clapton, Paul Simon — were wanting to meet with me. Some of them making demands, some of them complaining. There was tremendous anxiety at the company about how it was going to function. All of this was covered extensively in the media. In that context this Pavement release was a really minor thing. I loved Chris and Gerard. I wanted to be faithful to that relationship and I did the best I could to do that. It's very possible there were meetings that I was not at where somebody said that. I had five hundred people reporting to me. I was kind of the magnet that brought it there but, you know, I wasn't at every meeting.

I asked about Range Life. Stone Temple Pilots were an Atlantic band. They were pulling in millions. Crooked Rain had Atlantic distribution and marketing muscle behind it. Stephen Malkmus was talking shit about an Atlantic band on what was essentially an Atlantic co-release. Goldberg shrugged it off.

— I thought it was funny. At a major label you have so many different artists with different points of view. And at that time rock and roll was so fragmented in terms of different notions of what was cool and what was real. It didn't cause any great drama internally. I don't remember Stone Temple Pilots complaining about it and if they had it would have been too bad. Nobody told Stone Temple Pilots what lyrics to write and no one was going to tell Pavement what lyrics to write. I think it was just like water off a duck's back.

Our talk wound down. Goldberg brought it back to his alleged outburst.

— I just completely deny that I ever would have said anything negative about Pavement. I put them on a pedestal. I knew how important they were to people I respected. I myself like their music. I can absolutely believe that there were other people at both Atlantic and Warners who were not excited about Pavement because they didn't make radio hits and therefore they saw a ceiling to their sales. A lot of executives were programmed and directed to focus on hits. I can believe that there were other people there that would've said, great what am I supposed to do with this? But I would never have said that. It's very possible that I might have seemed and been preoccupied. It's totally impossible I would have felt or said anything dismissive or negative about them. Because I really, really respected and liked them.

I believed Goldberg. He seemed sincere. Plus how could he dig Sonic Youth and Nirvana and be that down on Pavement? I mulled over our conversation. Some things leapt out at me. The chairman of Atlantic gives Matador to Goldberg post-Crooked Rain — the time when the majors were said to be red hot for Pavement. Goldberg expresses affection for Cosloy, Lombardi et al. but admits Wowee Zowee's release — in context — was a blip. Scott Kannberg confirms the major-label stuff was hype. Stone Temple Pilots — who took endless shit from critics and indie people throughout the 90s and beyond, who could have called Danny Goldberg and said who the fuck is Pavement and what's this about? — STP rolls with the Range Life jibe. Billy Corgan — widely admired at the time — throws a fit. Ergo: Pavement weren't the coveted property their legend suggests. Scott Weiland et al. are probably okay guys. Billy Corgan is a world-class creep.

Five or six years ago I was at Great Jones Cafe, one of my favorite restaurants in New York. My friends and I had just been seated. I glanced across the small room. Mark Ibold was behind the bar pouring drinks. I knew he worked at Great Jones but hadn't seen him there before. I regressed a little, became a gaping fan. The bass player of my favorite band was standing just a few feet away. I nudged my friend Jim. He stared too. Our dinner companions were square. They didn't know who Pavement was or get the big deal. Half a beer later I relaxed and quit staring so much. But seeing Mark Ibold still blew my mind.

Ibold was a quieter presence in Pavement. He doesn't show up in a ton of interviews. He never said much onstage. But watching him could be as fun as watching Bob. Ibold has this great smile. He grins a lot playing live. He seems to be at once off in his own orbit and totally present. I was at a Pavement show once where late in the set Malkmus had to stop and reacquaint Ibold with an older number — Grave Architecture maybe? When Ibold had it down he turned to the crowd and smiled bashfully. He hopped a few steps. It was totally charming.

When Malkmus's first solo record came out there was an article in Time Out New York. David Berman was quoted. He said Malkmus solo was a happier person. He said the singing on Pavement records was informed by Malkmus's disgust at his bandmates' incompetence. He said disgust was the source of tension and sass that made Malkmus sound so entertainingly rude. He said the rudeness was gone now and whimsy was what's left. I've never met David Berman but these quotes make him sound like a major asshole — especially since two of these so-called incompetents were old friends of his who'd played on Silver Jews records. But never mind that — I remember reading Berman's comments thinking that's a shitty thing to say about Mark Ibold. There's some great bass lines on Brighten the Corners — Transport Is Arranged, Type Slowly, Blue Hawaiian. And after Malkmus, Ibold pulled off the sweetest second act. In 2006 he began playing with Sonic Youth. He joined initially as their touring bassist and later became a studio member of the band, making his recording debut on their album The Eternal. When I spoke to Ibold he was unfailingly modest. He told me Sonic Youth is still basically doing their own thing and that his input is on the same level as their sound man or lighting person. I mentioned the Brighten the Corners bass lines I like. He said he never thought of Pavement songs in terms of his bass playing. He said he tends to think of songs — all songs — not in terms of their component parts but how they sound as a whole.

I asked about going to Memphis for Wowee Zowee. Ibold said he was fuzzy on the details. His memory was jumbled and he couldn't put it all together at this point. Doug Easley and Davis McCain — the engineers — were great guys. Memphis was a blast. The barbecue was fantastic. I said barbecue seemed to be a running theme. He said it was no joke. Two places in particular — Cozy Corner and Payne's — fueled the band there. Cozy Corner had these great ribs. Payne's made great barbecue sandwiches. Their buddy Sherman Willmott turned them on to the good spots.

Ibold said maybe there was a bit more pressure after Crooked Rain. They'd all thought Slanted and Enchanted was huge — and then Crooked Rain made them even bigger. The other guys felt pressure but of course Stephen was the main songwriter and maybe he didn't feel it. Maybe in his mind he was just going along doing his thing.

— Stephen was the secret weapon of Pavement. And it's not even a secret. He always had so many songs that sounded so good to all of us. I actually joined the band as a fan of the band. I felt like I was a fan of the band as I was in the band. What happened most of the time before these records came out was that Steve would in some way give us an idea, whether it was at soundchecks or in practices. Mostly I remember getting cassettes of stuff that he'd fiddled around with at home. Sometimes he would just do stuff on a keyboard or a synthesizer or something. I would get these really weird, freaky versions, they were sort of skeletal versions of songs. And then we would all get together and work out different parts. And for me it was pretty simple. I would just normally follow along and play a bass line that was very similar to the low parts of his guitar lines. And I think that everyone else would kind of do the same thing. Scott would generally have one or two songs. Those were normally a little more straightforward, songs that I would be able to pick up immediately. I would say that Stephen's songs changed a lot while we worked on them. Sometimes he would have to adjust them to our ability levels. Which is probably something that is very nice for him now, playing in a band with really good musicians. He can probably just come up with anything and those guys can give him one better or whatever. But that was basically the deal. Things got worked out in the studio a lot. I felt like that was sometimes a waste of time, that we didn't prepare enough to go into the studio. But now actually after just doing Sonic Youth stuff in the studio I realized that not everyone does do a lot of preparation beforehand. A lot of times everything happens in the studio.

— Is that how Sonic Youth works?

— On this last album that I worked with them on, yeah. We rehearsed once or twice then went into the studio and did a bunch of versions of the songs we rehearsed and then picked the ones that were the best. Pavement kind of did that but it would take longer. A lot of the corrections would happen in the studio. I was always conscious of the clock ticking in the studio and thinking, oh my god, we're paying for this and we're fucking up right now. I think one of the reasons we were considered to be this slacker rock band is that sometimes we would just say, look this is done, this is good the way it is. A lot of the times the result — whether it was fucked up or not — would be great. I think that's one of the reasons that a lot of the Pavement records have that charm that a lot of people respond to. They're not overworked.

Ibold dismissed the Wowee Zowee-as-career-killer talk.

— To us what sounded like interesting songs or types of songs or a sequence of songs that would make up an album might not have been the thing that everybody was so interested in. And maybe for some reason on the previous two records people were more willing to get into that. Although Wowee Zowee did end up being Pavement fans' favorite record, I would say. Challenging people is fine. But we didn't want it to be difficult listening. We were hoping to blow people's minds with every record that we came out with. I remember after each record being super excited about some of the songs and being like, wow we're doing something that's really new, there's no one else doing this right now. I think everyone felt that way. It's probably a normal feeling for people in a band to have. I'm a pretty picky person and I still felt that way on every record, for a few songs at least. I think that if a record has one or two songs that you feel that way about on it, it's worth putting out.

It was early evening. I was stretched on the couch. I stared at the wall and tried clearing my mind of all thoughts. I'd had two beers and was nursing a third. The phone rang — Doug Easley calling from Memphis. Easley and I had been playing phone tag for a week or so. I didn't know if he was calling to schedule something or if this was it.

— Do you want to talk now? I asked.

— Well I've got about a fifteen-minute drive ahead of me.

I thought for a second. I was a little high from the beers. — All right. This is sort of unexpected but let me grab my stuff and we'll do it.

— That's how I like to work, said Easley.

I walked to the kitchen and set up my gear on the table. I opened my notebook and flipped to the right page. Doug Easley led me through his background.

— I've had studios since the late 70s. I got involved with the underbelly of Memphis, you might say. Alex

Chilton and all those guys, they would go to the big cities and make contact with people out of town, the underground scene, Lydia Lunch or whoever, you know. Alex would hang out with a bunch of people. Then we'd record some of their records, or Alex would bring bands like the Gories down from Detroit. I was sort of the do-it-yourself guy in town. I had a studio behind my house, which was one of few at the time. I actually started recording as a kid, back in grade school, like in fifth grade. We were making tapes back in those days, sort of weird little radio dramas. This was like 1968. We had a little band called the White River Catfish. We'd beat on pots and pans. My buddy's brother was in the Box Tops, so he had a lot of guitars laying around and we'd try and play instruments. But after my college days and beyond I had studios off and on in various places. The Grifters had a lot to do with going out of town and spreading the word. Occasionally I'd make stickers. I would go out and play with various people and take stickers around. And then it sort of just blossomed. There was a rash of bands around the time Pavement came here. Sonic Youth, Wilco, the Blues Explosion. Jeff Buckley might have been a little later, I guess. But a lot of those bands. And then all the fans of all of those bands that had bands. So it was coast to coast. It was pretty nutty.

— As far as Pavement was there any kind of preproduction work? Did you know what kind of record they were going to make when they showed up?

— No. Hell no. I don't know if they knew what they were gonna do.

Easley laughed. — I don't think they had rehearsed at

all. They'd all come from different areas and convened at the studio as far as I can remember. I don't have the best memory in the world. They seemed to be extremely off the cuff and it was very invigorating in that way. It was like, wow you don't have to worry about anything. Just go do it. That's what it felt like. Lyrics were changing. Every time you'd try to take a vocal it'd be a different lyric. It was very experimental-feeling in the beginning stages and then some overdubs would happen. It was so loose. It was very loose.

— So it was a good pairing then, in terms of the way you like to work?

— Yeah it was very inspiring to me. Because you see so many people just beat the hell out of it. And that doesn't always work. Stephen, he just seemed like he was blowin in the wind, you know. He's just like, as free as the wind will blow.

He laughed. — They started out in a strange manner, very elemental. Two and three people recording at a time. Basically like being at practice and going Here's a song. There were some ensemble things but it was mainly like a practice — Stephen introducing new songs to the other bandmates. I don't think anybody knew what the hell was going down. That's the way I remember it.

— How'd you end up playing pedal steel on Father to a Sister of Thought?

— Oh probably somebody just asked. There was probably a pedal steel sittin in the room and they said hey man, that'd be cool if you got on there. That's probably the way that went down. I don't remember a ton of things because I was just sort of hustling. We were all just hustling to get it done.

The studio's biggest projects in terms of record sales came later on. The White Stripes and Modest Mouse worked on gold and platinum records at Easley. Jack White mixed Van Lear Rose, the Loretta Lynn record, there. In 2005 the studio was destroyed in a fire. Easley and McCain reopened in another building but the pace isn't as hectic. In the old days they booked bands one after the other. In the old days they put in long days and nights. Easley still has the original tapes of a lot of those records. They were in a concrete room and survived the blaze.

— There's tapes everywhere, he said. — I've got tapes up the wazoo. And they'll never be touched again I'm sure.

Easley had arrived where he was going. Birds chirped in the background. I pictured him out in the country somewhere. I thanked him for his time and we hung up. I got a beer from the fridge and walked back to the couch. Three minutes later the phone rang. It was Doug Easley. Something else had come to him — Steve West painting little Civil War men. West would sit in the studio and paint these plastic toy soldiers when he was done recording his parts. Easley always remembered that. He gathered a few of the soldiers and put them in the studio shrine. It began as a Django Reinhardt shrine and became a place for those who'd recorded there to leave a little mark. The shrine was in the hallway outside the control room. I thanked Easley again. We got off the phone. I lay back on the couch and drank the beer. My mind wandered. A light bulb flicked on: Scott Kannberg's tune Painted Soldiers.

The names Doug Easley and Davis McCain appear in the credits to a small handful of my favorite records: Extra Width by the Jon Spencer Blues Explosion, Under the Bushes Under the Stars by Guided by Voices, Don't Ask Don't Tell by Come. Another name pops up a lot — Bryce Goggin. Goggin produced and mixed Don't Ask Don't Tell. He produced and engineered tracks on Ride the Fader by Chavez, a fantastic record now largely unsung. He mixed Crooked Rain and Wowee Zowee. He co-recorded and mixed Brighten the Corners. I met Goggin at Trout Recording, his studio in Park Slope Brooklyn. It was April Fool's Day, cool and overcast. Goggin cut his teeth at two Manhattan studios, Sound on Sound and Baby Monster. When Baby Monster started it was at 645 Broadway, close to the old Knitting Factory and CBGB. Baby Monster was cheap. A lot of Knitting Factory and CB's bands would work there. By the time Pavement arrived Baby Monster had relocated to Fourteenth Street and upgraded to a Neve board.

— This was around the time of Crooked Rain?

— Yeah. That's when I first met Steve and the band. This woman Janet Billig — and I only heard this second-hand — was sort of like advising Steve in the hopes of getting to manage him and Pavement. She pointed him towards Baby Monster and me to mix Crooked Rain.

— Don't you play on the record too?

— I played piano on Range Life. I might have, you know, rattled something else. Those guys are very stream-of-consciousness people so we didn't really think about who did what. We just kind of did it.

— What did the work on Wowee Zowee entail?

— It took longer to mix that record. I think we did more tracking than on Crooked Rain. I remember cutting a few vocals on Crooked Rain but I may have cut about half the vocals on Wowee Zowee. There were overdubs to do. There was a list of things to do — including Rattled by the Rush, which we definitely did the guitar solo on. Wowee Zowee was maybe two-thirds tracked by the time it came to me. All the basics were done at Easley.

— How was that different from Crooked Rain?

— It was a little bit more involved. Wowee Zowee was less complete when it came to me in some ways. But Crooked Rain was actually fucked in terms of the professionalism of its recording. They had gone to this place at 251 West Thirtieth Street with this guy Mark Venezia, who had an understanding of recording but really kind of dabbled.

Goggin cataloged the fuckups: no track sheets for any of the songs, no leader tape between songs, sound quality going to shit as the recording progressed. He said Mark Venezia had been a salesman at Rogue Music and was probably still there. I'd been trying to locate Venezia — the Wowee Zowee credits list a four-day session with him in February of 94. The Easley session went down that November. I made a note to check Rogue Music. Goggin continued.

— I had never seen anybody be so uninhibited about making their record. Especially during Crooked Rain but also Wowee Zowee. We would cut vocals and we would do them in one pass and Stephen would be reading off a sheet of paper some vague ideas of what the vocals would be. And if we were gonna punch the vocal it would be only because he didn't like the lyric. It wasn't because he didn't like the read at all. Which was a far cry from the arduous process of cutting five tracks of a song with a singer and going line by line and cobbling them together — which was and still is a pretty normal routine in the studio.

— That's what Doug Easley said when I spoke to him. He said it was inspiring because Pavement worked so loosely. They didn't overthink things.

— And it sounded great. I remember when I was recording Brighten the Corners, that was the first time I had been in the studio with the band. It was totally magical and infectious. The Nast — I had never seen that in action before.

— The what?

— Bob Nastanovich.

— Right.

— He was like, what key should I press on the keyboard? And Malkmus would be like, ah that one and that one and that one'll be good. And he would just go at it.

— Is that how they worked on Brighten the Corners? Because that's a much tighter record.

— Yeah I mean that record, I cut it. I had actually been producing records for about two or three years by the time I did Brighten the Corners so I had preconceptions about the way things should work. So in spite of Pavement's looseness there was some dick standing around —

He laughed. — And there were retakes and edits made on basic tracks that I'd never seen before on some of the other stuff. Getting back to Wowee Zowee, I definitely felt there was a little bit of the shadow of success hanging over us all. Including myself. I had been really enamored with the outcome of Crooked Rain and, you know, when it came time to mix Wowee Zowee there I was basking in the sunshine of success. Why did I want to actually try and repeat it? So there was a little bit of that energy.

— Do you think the band felt that as well?

— Yeah. There was a little taint of that, I think. It didn't seem to be in the Brighten the Corners experience at all. You know, counter to the pop formula of trying to repeat oneself Malkmus always wanted to do something differently. That was something that he and I both spoke about the importance of. You don't want to do the same record every time. You want to do things differently. The fact that he worked with me for three records is kind of counter to that philosophy. But we did come up with different environments every time. There was this attempt to reinvent every time. Every time. That was his critical way to keep things fresh.

— And he was always the one steering the ship in terms of how the band was going to sound?

— There was never an I Have This Vision conversation with anybody. It was always organic. There was a very in-the-moment sense of what the music needed to make it work. I didn't have a star chart out. There was no grand design. There was, I've written this many songs and we're gonna work on them and see how they go together and that's the way it's done. The guy had five paragraphs on a piece of paper and he would choose two of them to sing the lyrics from and then go Yeah man, that's good. Ship? Whatever. The ship was in his head floating around and he was just searching for it.

Our talk wound down. Goggin showed me a guitar, a red Gibson SG Standard with P-90 pickups. Malkmus used it to play the solo on Rattled by the Rush.

— Actually when we were doing it he was just monitoring through that.

He pointed to a small Sony boombox that looked many years old.

— Which is pretty funny because it's such a ripping thing. Malkmus did it in a low-key way. The guitar amp was in another room and we were in the control room listening on this fucking thing really quietly. And he was just slaying it, you know. This after I'd spent years in control rooms with guitar players who are like, please turn it up till I die! I gotta feel it!

Stephen Malkmus jumped up a league chops-wise on Wowee Zowee. Rattled by the Rush was clear evidence of greater gifts. The progression continued through his time in Pavement — killer solos on Fin and The Hexx, from Brighten the Corners and Terror Twilight, respectively. His solo work grooves on some other level. Starting with Pig Lib — his second record with the Jicks, a more proficient group of players — the songs grew longer, their arrangements more complex, the solos more mind-blowing. Malkmus achieved this without sacrificing basic pleasures. He still wrote strong melodies, choruses and hooks. He mixed epic jams with shorter pop numbers — Baby C'mon and Gardenia, from Face the Truth and Real Emotional Trash, respectively. The leap between his playing in early Pavement and the Jicks is astonishing. I had mentioned this when I was talking to Bob. Bob had said, yeah if you go see him live you'll hear a lot of that fucking guitar. Then he'd laughed and said:

— Pavement edited Stephen to an extent as well. I'm not saying that he would go out of bounds or something like that. But I think one of the reasons he enjoys playing with the people he plays with now is that he is completely free. Whereas in Pavement, not only could we not keep up with him, we certainly didn't want to. The songs are simpler and more straightforward. There were a few songs on Wowee Zowee that got jammed out. Pueblo if it was played right would be a long jammy song. Half a Canyon would get real jammy. That song was good. But that's the kind of music Stephen's into. Those are his heroes and that's what he's going to play like. I can't imagine Pavement making a whole album of ten-minute songs.

I called Rogue Music and asked for Mark Venezia. A guy who sounded Australian told me he didn't work there anymore. I asked if he knew how I could get in touch with him. The guy asked who I was. I told him my name and that I was writing a book. He took down my number. I thanked him and hung up. Venezia called ten minutes later. I ran through my spiel. He said you know it's funny, in all this time you're the first person to contact me about Pavement. I said that was sort of odd seeing as how he recorded their biggest record. He said yeah well I'm glad that you called.

Everyone who worked at Rogue Music had to have

a nickname. Mark Venezia chose Maverick, after the reckless, Righteous Brothers-crooning hero of Top Gun. But his boss hated that movie and instead gave Venezia a choice between Dead Meat, Wash Out or Walleye — each a reference to the Top Gun spoof Hot Shots. Venezia chose Walleye. The store was on the tenth floor of a dark building on West Thirtieth Street. It was one of the go-to spots for vintage gear. The rest of the building was rehearsal studios. When one opened up on the eighth floor Venezia snagged it and started building a recording studio there. He mentioned this to his friend Tom Surgal. Surgal mentioned this band Pavement. Venezia had never heard of them. Surgal set up a meeting. Stephen Malkmus dropped by, maybe Mark Ibold too. Venezia played a track he'd been working on. Malkmus said yeah fine, we'll work here. It happened quickly. The studio wasn't even done.

— But because of that chaos, said Venezia, — because it just wasn't ready yet I think that there was a lot of experimentation that happened that really helped create the sound of the Crooked Rain and Wowee Zowee sessions. And also the fact that I had like fifteen vintage guitar amps that I had been collecting from Rogue Music.

— What was it like making Crooked Rain?

— Oh it was great. It was just a really nice vibe. Basically I was hooking things up as we went. It was funny because you'd be done at the end of the day and Steve would be like, hey if you wanna lay some tracks down go ahead. Go ahead and play around with it. He was totally cool about stuff like that. I think I did a couple things, a background vocal on one track and a scream on

Fillmore Jive. I didn't get to know Scott that well. Scott was there for most of the recording but then he was gone for a while. But I'll tell you, the most fun I had was on AT&T. That was a blast. I think all of Crooked Rain was pretty much done and obviously the Wowee Zowee tracks that I worked on —

— So hold on. You did Crooked Rain and then they got in touch with you a while later to record some new tracks?

— No. These tracks were all done at once. It wasn't like a year later they did Wowee Zowee. This was all done during one session.

— So the songs you recorded that ended up on Wowee Zowee were done during Crooked Rain?

— Exactly. They were extra tracks. I remember Grounded specifically. It had such a magical sound to it. When it didn't end up on Crooked Rain I was like, oh my god that's the best song, how could they not put that on the album? And then of course later on they put it on Wowee Zowee.

The Random Falls version of Grounded turned up officially on Everything Is Nice, Matador's tenth-anniversary compilation, mislabeled a Slanted and Enchanted outtake. Five years later it was included on the Crooked Rain reissue. The earlier version is faster, jumpier, sloppier — half the song it would eventually become. I told Venezia they'd reworked Grounded at Easley. I asked if he was sure about the one-session thing. Yes, he said, with the exception of AT&T. That was done a few weeks after the Crooked Rain sessions and that was all Stephen. What happened was Venezia was working in the store. It was the middle of the afternoon. Stephen called and said he wanted to record a track. Did Venezia have time? He may have mentioned something about a solo project. Venezia said sure. He met Stephen downstairs. They recorded and mixed AT&T in two hours. Stephen played every instrument and did all the vocals. Venezia was blown away.

— It was this amazing song that came to life in front of your eyes within a two-hour period. That was a really good time, just to produce something that sounded so cool so quickly. You could see when Stephen was working, he had a knack. You could just tell. I've worked with a lot of bands since that time and very rarely do you see someone like that in the studio who creates something like that, knows it and is content to move on. When we were doing Crooked Rain they were definitely a band but you could tell Stephen was the creative force. There was no doubt about that. But everyone was cool with it. I think in part because it was such a kickass record. You could tell what was unfolding within like a week.

— Had you ever done a full-length project before?

— No.

— Wow. It seems crazy in retrospect that you undertook that. Maybe crazy in a good way, I don't know.

— Well you know it's funny. I didn't realize the magnitude of it until a couple months later. But I knew when we were recording it that they were great songs. I felt like, okay this is gonna be a good record. I could tell there was something bigger happening than I first realized.

I mentioned that Bryce Goggin said the Crooked Rain tapes were . . . amateur. Venezia had heard and read similar comments over the years. It bummed him out but he didn't want to get into any kind of weird back and forth. He insisted the core sound of the recording was good. He said, I know guitar sounds and there's some great ones on Crooked Rain. The Rogue Music pieces were crucial to that. He'd filled Random Falls — this quasi-crash-pad studio — with vintage guitar amps, tube mics, mic pres. He ran a lengthy gearhead riff. They used an Ampeg Reverberocket on Stop Breathin. One of Venezia's favorites. It had a beautiful tremolo sound and tracked beautifully to tape. They also used Danelectros, Premiers, Univoxes. Malkmus played a twelve-string Rickenbacker on Gold Soundz. He played a battered Ibanez acoustic on Range Life. It was this cheap guitar just sitting around the studio. But it sounded right with the microphone — an AKG C 26A — and a Demeter mic pre. It's all about the chain, said Venezia, and that chain was correct. The Range Life vocal was tricky. They used this old mic pre, a Telefunken V72, a relic from the Beatles' EMI days. But it's actually a line amp, very hot. Venezia placed another pre in front of it to reduce the gain. A bit ghetto but still — the vocal sound on Range Life is one of the best on the record. They should have used that chain on more songs. Stuff like that happened a lot. They'd hit on these sweet spots just fucking around, trying unorthodox combinations, seeing what sounded best. The band had plenty of room to experiment. Without that experimentation Crooked Rain wouldn't be the same. Venezia kept talking. My mind jumped around. I thought of Strings of Nashville, a Gold Soundz b-side. One of the slow sad ones. Pavement's great at those. I was pretty sure it was a Random Falls tune. I made a note to double check. I've always loved the guitar tone on Strings of Nashville. There's an instrumental version on the Crooked Rain reissue. Even listening to that one gets me. In the reissue booklet Scott Kannberg says the guitar sounds on Newark Wilder are some of the best of all time. I agree. But could those be conjured strictly by triage work in the mix? Maybe now with Pro Tools but on a micro-budget recording in 93/94? Also in the booklet Malkmus says he feels bad calling Venezia co-engineer in the original credits and admits that Walleye did the lion's share of the work. I asked Venezia if he'd seen that. He said yeah that was cool, that was a nice thing to hear. He said he knew he fucked some basic things up and was sure mixing the record was a lot work. Bryce did a great job, there's no question about that. Venezia stuck to polite phrasings and kept his responses high-road. I caught the subtext: no magic wand's going to turn a shit recording into Crooked Rain. The right sounds have to be captured on tape in the first place.

I sat at the kitchen table with my notebook in front of me. The recording gizmos were connected. I was ready to go. The appointed time arrived. I took a deep breath. I waited exactly three minutes, entered the number and pressed send. It was a heavy call to be making. I flashed on countless nights in my room getting lost in that voice . . . singing along in the car as I drove through lake-effect snowstorms on back roads in Michigan . . . a night in Grand Rapids coming up on twelve years ago. Whatever, he said. This is a tune called Grounded, he said. Stephen Malkmus had cast a spell over my entire adult life. He was in his yard in Portland Oregon raking when I called.

— The first thing I wanted to ask about is the recording chronology. Mark Venezia told me that all the Random Falls songs that ended up on Wowee Zowee — aside from AT&T — were done during the Crooked Rain sessions in 93. Is that the case?

— It's hard to know, said Malkmus, — but some of those things, I really think they were after. But maybe not before Crooked Rain was out or even mixed. Maybe there's something on Wowee Zowee that's not. But I think it was just b-sides and messing-around time, you know, because the whole band wasn't there. It was just me and Steve West and Mark Ibold. Usually Kannberg was sitting around. Like during Crooked Rain he was there. But I don't think he was there for the other session.

— So you guys could have been recording in February of 94 right as Crooked Rain was coming out?

— Yeah. Mark still had his studio and he had some new pieces. He was always getting new stuff from where he worked up above at this secondhand place. And it was that and the combination of going back down to Easley Recording where we did most of the songs, I guess, except for Fight This Generation — well Brinx Job was from the Crooked Rain session. But the others aren't. They're after.

— When you were recording those other songs did you think you were making songs for another album or were you just working on miscellaneous tracks?

— Yeah just miscellaneous tracks. Or weirder songs that I didn't have to explain to anybody and I could just kind of like play them even more off the cuff. Which we did a little on Crooked Rain. I guess Steve West and I rehearsed a little bit for that in his loft. But this time we were just going to Mark's — he was charging twenty, thirty bucks an hour and I think we had extra tape left over from Crooked Rain. So I think we were just working on b-sides. I don't really know what the plan was. It was definitely going to be not as standard as Crooked Rain, the songs that we were doing. Not that they're totally avant garde. But it was just a little bit weirder.

— Did Crooked Rain exceed your expectations for what you hoped to achieve with the band?

— Yeah. I mean it starts more with the one before that. That's the one that really was the surprising one — Slanted and Enchanted — that it was in mainstream media and that people were actually sort of interested beyond the fanzine culture. So that was like, oh things are changing a little bit. But then with Crooked Rain Matador had a deal with a major label and they were going to release it to a bigger audience. But we didn't get a producer or make mixes for radio or something like that. We were just going to mix it ourselves. There was no conscious effort to be on radio and MTV. Maybe there was a conscious effort to make more poppy songs, with more bass and a fuller sound and some different references that were more accessible. But not in the way that it's really done. You know like you get Andy Wallace to do it or you get Butch Vig. That's the way that you really do it. You get a manager and you put yourself out there and get Spike Jonze to do your video. We hadn't planned that far ahead. But what you said, when it did get more — when there was Cut Your Hair and all of a sudden there was this alternative nation, I guess that was surprising. We didn't expect to be part of it.

— And you toured that whole year for the record, right?

— Probably. We toured a lot. We were young and wanted to go see the world. We were really excited, as most young bands are, to be part of something that we didn't know where it was gonna end.

— Do you like touring?

— Yeah. I mean we overdid it a bit. But I did like it. Touring is a very childlike thing. People take care of you a bit. And you have a purpose and you feel wanted and all these things that children want.

— Speaking of children is it harder to tour now, being away from your kids?

— Yeah it's harder. But I don't go very often. I still like it. I take it for what it is, like a chance to just be selfish a little bit, sleep in or something. You're not supposed to think of touring as sleeping in. You're supposed to stay out till three and get up at five. But it's easier than having two young kids. The needs of the others are just, be in the van at this time and be at soundcheck on time and remember the lyrics.

— Were you writing songs on the Crooked Rain tour?

— Maybe some riffs. But not lyrics. I never really tried to do that. Some people do that — they write on little scraps of paper and they're really driven. At least I imagine some people do that.

— Making songs at soundcheck and stuff like that.

— Yeah I've heard of bands that do that. Maybe we did that a little bit but not like it was one of our goals. We didn't really write songs together anyway, we never did. Sometimes I'd play a riff and then if it sounded good I'd go We can play that, stow that away as a future thing to do.

— So you write at home typically?

— Yeah at home. When there was a home. Back then I didn't really have a home. I was just a couch surfer. I lived at Steve West's. I had an apartment in Greenpoint for a while. It was a really nice studio. Big windows, really pretty. David Berman got it first. He lived there first and I took it over from him.

— Is that where you came after the Crooked Rain tour? Or did you ever really get off tour?

— Not for long. I was probably just staying at Steve West's. I was still working at the Whitney a little bit. They took me back on in between tours because they knew that I was gonna be part time.

— Why the decision to go to Easley so quickly after the Crooked Rain period?

— I don't remember how fast it was. It just seemed like it was time to make a record, like we had the songs and it was time to go to the next thing. That place is great. There was a Memphis kind of cult — this band the Grifters had recorded there. They were emissaries for the studio. The two guys that run it — Doug and Davis — they're really down-to-earth southern guys. They were kind of surprised by this new world of indie and open to it. They didn't have any aspirations to be a major-label recording studio. I think they were just doing it by the seat of their pants. It was affordable. Nice echo chamber. Mellotron. They had a couple of amps, not a whole lot. Big room. Eventually a lot of groups went there. Sonic Youth went there and recorded Washing Machine. There's a lot of history in Memphis. You could hope it would rub off on you. The spirit of Stax/Volt and I guess Elvis to a lesser extent, for me. But other people would be interested in Sun Records. Big Star of course. They were from there.

— Part of the Pavement mythology is that you guys spent that period fielding and turning down major-label offers — that everyone was clamoring to sign the band.

— I had some meetings. It wasn't out of control because we didn't have a manager and we weren't actively fielding offers. But we went on tour with Sonic Youth and we met Gary Gersh, who was then a star A&R guy with Geffen. He had signed Nirvana and Sonic Youth and I think Beck. So there was maybe a time when we could have gone with him and over to Gold Mountain, Danny Goldberg's management company. But we decided not to get a manager. That was a fork in the road where I guess we could have gone another way and gone over to Geffen and tried to be a little bit more mainstream in terms of having a force behind the band. But besides the fact that we were scared or skeptical of committing to that route — because there was still the feeling that if you did that they would get you a producer and water down the band and try to make it more commercial, we were worried about that — besides that fact we really liked the people at Matador and we knew we could probably get by without a manager and just do it ourselves still. We got some offers in England from big labels. Rick Rubin's label gave us a contract, I remember.

— American?

— Yeah. That's the only contract I actually got that was a full contract that said come to our label. It was big and it was a very long commitment. We were gonna be with them forever. Rick Rubin, I respect him and his ear. There's something about him, some kind of mysticism. That kind of LA almost old-school mysticism that he's got around him. There must be something there. He must be smart and talented. And he's definitely posi-tive, he's trying to generate good vibes. Nevertheless we just were like, these Matador guys, I think this is where we belong. We were a little skeptical. That being said, American had some success with the Black Crowes. But there were a lot of misses by the label, I think. There was maybe a question of, are they a responsible concern or is it just a plaything for Rick while he's producing? He was probably just starting the Johnny Cash thing then. But they had Slayer. If I had to say there was a metal band I liked it would be Slayer. I don't like metal at all. There's no groove to it. Rarely. Even the new kind of black metal that's cool now. It's not my bag of tricks. I guess I could go see some of it. But there's only so much time.

— You said earlier that you were thinking Wowee Zowee would be if not avant garde then at least more off the cuff. Is that the direction you knew you were gonna take it?

— I think, yeah. It was maybe a reaction to Crooked Rain. That was somewhat conservative. There's weird stuff on there, I guess, by some people's standards. It was experimental in the sense that we didn't know what we were doing and didn't know what our sound was. So almost anything we did was an experiment in a certain way, even if we were trying to do a country rock song. But yeah, Wowee Zowee was gonna be less planned out. There's a lot of songs that have basically no lyrics, like Extradition and Brinx Job and Best Friend's Arm and Half a Canyon. They're just me projecting rock and roll id or attitude. You know what I mean? Some of the songs have real clear words. I guess there's a split. Some of the songs are angular and somewhat about the sound and the experiments of the recording and some of them — the ones we did at Easley — those were more like a band, Rattled by the Rush, We Dance, Blackout. Those three and Grounded and Grave Architecture. Pueblo doesn't really have lyrics, that's maybe more like R.E.M.'s first album or something, where Michael Stipe didn't have the lyrics ready and that's why people think it's mysterious. He might have consciously said, I don't wanna have the lyrics ready — or he just didn't have the lyrics ready. With most bands you work the song out and kind of sing along and try to convince the band it's good before you have the lyrics. Like why waste the effort to make them. I don't have like a novel of lyrics sitting around. Most people don't.

— I got the sense that the lyrics on Brighten the Corners were more crafted.

— Yeah. That was maybe taking a break from Wowee Zowee or saying, well let's be more formalist. Something tugging back in that other direction. I'm sure I was thinking something like that. I haven't really thought about the fact that there aren't that many lyrics on Wowee Zowee. Or that they're not very — they're just kind of impressionistic. When I think about it now it really is very slapdash.

Malkmus laughed. — But in a good way.

— Did you make up lyrics in the booth? Or did you have a piece of paper with some notes on it or something, a loose guide?

— Well some of them, like Best Friend's Arm and Half a Canyon and Pueblo, there was no lyric sheet. I think I was just kind of emoting in there. But Grounded and Rattled by the Rush and We Dance, there's definitely — I can see a lyric sheet in my hand of some sort. You can kind of tell if you hear that I'm mumbling more or you really can't make any sense of it — if you hear that there either weren't many lyrics or there was just a chorus or something.

— What were some of your personal influences at the time?

— For the lyrics, I can't remember. But I'd try to make some of the songs be influenced by mainstream things that I didn't really care that much about but that we were kind of a bastard version of. So the first song is kind of like a Bowie singing style. I'm not much of a fan of Bowie's but I like a couple of songs. The second song is kind of a Led Zeppelin riff. Another band that when push comes to shove I really don't like. I like Dazed and Confused and some of the hits. There's probably like six songs I actually really like and the rest just is kind of boring to me. I don't know if it's because they're popular. But it's not — because I always like to listen to the Stones, for instance. I like Emotional Rescue and Exile on Main Street. Maybe not the last couple albums but I just really like them. I like Mick Jagger's singing. I don't really like Robert Plant's singing and I don't like the bombast of some of their generic blues. That being said, there's six Led Zeppelin songs that I'm blown away by and I admire their craft. And then the next song, that Blackout one, I don't remember what that would have been. It's kind of R.E.M.-y, I guess, but not really. Brinx Job, I can't think of anything that's like. It's got like a Ween-style thing to it maybe. But I didn't really listen to Ween.

— I always thought Brinx Job sounded like a studio jam. But you said it had been recorded a while before.

— Yeah I'm sure it was done on Crooked Rain.

— Was that a written song or was it more of a jam?

— I wrote the guitar parts. It's kind of a jazz progression. I thought it was nice. I can't think of anything it's like really. It's just kind of warped. We had some warped b-sides in Pavement, just kind of stoner goofy songs. Then Extradition's kind of like channeling Royal Trux a little bit and a little Stones-y somehow. Best Friend's Arm is kind of like Beastie Boys, even though it doesn't sound like that I think I was trying — Serpentine Pad is kind of singing a little like the riot grrrls sing, Bikini Kill or something. It's actually produced like some kind of Butch Vig Dirty-era song. It's really compressed. I didn't plan on it being that way. The producer did that. He totally made it sound really Dirty-style. But I thought the chorus was kind of late-period Black Flag, their fake metal period. And then Grave Architecture's kind of jazzy. There's some riff that's like that from some other song. It was probably Grant Green. People sort of were into him at the time. Fight This Generation, the second half, is kind of Fall-y. The first half is just a waltz. I don't know what influences waltzes, they're all the same. You should only have one on your album probably but they're nice.

— The early version of Pueblo sounds like the Beach Boys.

— Yup. That was an idea to do that the first time, the Beach Boys harmonies. But I can't really sing like that. Animal Collective does it better. Flux = Rad's kind of like an early Nirvana song, Bleach-era Nirvana. Half a Canyon is just a rock and roll Trux thing. The end is a little like Stereolab, an effort to make a drone. Scott's songs, you know, he's obviously got the Fall-influenced one, the last song. And Kennel District — that's his kind of song. I don't know what they're influenced by. They're just like nice-guy poppy songs, a little Pixie-ish. It's his style.

— I like that strange keyboard he's playing on it.

— Totally. He's good at finding keyboard sounds. He added a few of those on Wowee Zowee and the one before that.

— Did you mention Grounded?

— Grounded. Yeah I don't know what that is. It's Sonic Youth-y maybe. The guitar intro is at least. That's maybe a little like Kennel District — you don't know what it is because it's so simple in a certain way. There's no chord changes. It's the same thing all the way through with different permutations. I could never do that anymore.

— Do what, write that kind of song?

— Yeah. Like Summer Babe or In the Mouth a Desert — they don't have any chorus. The chorus is the same chords, just louder or quieter. I don't know how to do that anymore. I used to be able to.

— What do you recall about recording at Easley?

— I recall eating a lot of food and not getting that much done.

He laughed but stopped short of mentioning barbecue specifically.

— Or getting something done but having a lot of the songs not turn out well, so that's why we used different versions of them. Like we used the original Fight This Generation and AT&T and Flux = Rad — the ones

Steve and I did in New York. Then again Rattled by the Rush really turned out great. I remember being really psyched about that and spending a lot of time doing overdubs on it. And the We Dance song turned out to be kind of spooky and better than I thought. There was really no plan for that song. I don't remember too much, unfortunately. I don't think anyone does. I should more than anybody else. I think we were just drinking beer and eating twice a day and recording the standard twelve hours that you do but not really going over that and not worrying about if it sounded that good or not, just trusting that we could mix it. Because when we did Crooked Rain we didn't know what we were doing recording it. We didn't even have any help, or not as much. We had Mark Venezia, I don't want to underestimate him. And it turned out sounding good. So we just figured that's how it's always gonna be. When we got the rough mixes they sounded kind of flabby. It sounded okay but it sounded much better when Bryce Goggin mixed it.

— You're talking about Crooked Rain?

— Wowee Zowee too. It sounded much better after Bryce got his hands on it. I guess I just thought, well that's what always happens. But it's not the case sometimes. Sometimes you just recorded it bad or you go to a bad mixer who doesn't make it sound better. But Bryce was on a roll. He really clicked with us. So did the Easley guys and Mark Venezia in a way. But it was more hands-off, like some encouragement and good vibes but not major sonic architecture.

— So it wasn't like Doug Easley was saying, Stephen I think you should do that again.

— Yeah he doesn't really do that. But he'd be positive.

Malkmus mimicked a southern accent: — I don't know, that seemed a little slow, you might wanna do that again. Sometimes he would say that. When you're doing it you just want it to be over a little bit. You go in the control room to listen and hope it's good. This is after the magic, after you've done it a couple days in a studio and you're almost tired of it already. Sometimes there's more enthusiasm. You listen back and it obviously is good. Other times it maybe isn't but you just say that's good enough.

— Aside from AT&T are there any other songs on which you're playing multiple instruments, or all the instruments?

— Yeah. I would say I'm playing every instrument except drums on Rattled by the Rush. Maybe not bass. And the first song, We Dance. I think we all play on Blackout, maybe. But I play everything on Brinx Job and all the guitars on Grave Architecture and the bass, I bet. Maybe not, maybe Mark's on that. Pueblo, I think I'm all the guitars and all the bass on that. Mark might remember differently. I'm pretty sure I play everything on Half a Canyon and I definitely play everything on Fight This Generation except drums. Extradition and Best Friend's Arm, I play everything on those.

— So you play most of the guitars on the record?

— Yeah just about everything. Scott might be in there. On his songs he's in there. He might be jangling a bit. He plays some nice jangly guitar sometimes. But I'd have to go back and listen to see if it's actually on there.

— So what's he doing while you're recording guitar tracks?

— He's hanging out. Adding advice, saying that's good, maybe try something else. Or he's just messing around, drinking a beer. Like everybody else.

He laughed. — Mark was getting more and more into the band and playing more stuff. He got to know how I play more. I would think he probably played on Rattled by the Rush and Blackout. Maybe Grave Architecture and three or four more. I'm sure he played on Grounded. Scott's on Grounded too, he's gotta be. But there was some stuff where I would just play it because of the speed at which we were recording, just to move on. Or I'd have an idea to do a counterpoint thing. With songs you just learned it's easier to play to yourself than to have someone else play with you. Unfortunately it's a one-way street a little bit. It's like you have to follow the leader, not the other way around. Which makes it much harder for everybody else to play to their style.

— Did you play on Scott's songs?

— Yeah I play on there. Maybe not on the last song because that one's kind of weird. That might be just him. It's got a weird timing and he knew what he wanted on that. But I'm sure I'm on Kennel District because we all played that as a band before we recorded it.

— So there was kind of a Billy Corgan thing, picking up the instruments and banging out all the parts.

— Yeah but — I don't know. It got better after a while. It's just how we did it. We were moving fast. No one was completely feeling abused by it. It was more like, you know what you're doing, let's just get it done. We also were working towards maybe becoming more of a band, as we tried to do on Brighten the Corners.

— No, I get it. It wasn't some dictatorial prison.

— If they're not saying it was then I'm glad. I'm trying to imagine what Bob would say — maybe like Steve knew what he wanted to do and we just wanted it to be the best it could be. I hope that's what it was like.

— So the band dynamic was good during that period?

— Yeah. It was fine. Maybe for Steve West it was a little stressful. He was always on the spot a little bit trying to play his parts. Doing a great job when he did a great job but also sometimes . . . You know, he would get the blame even if it wasn't his fault, if a song wasn't that groovy. It's not fair but that was a time in rock when people were really hard on drummers, I think. People still get on them. They're constantly being judged. Singers I guess would be too. But bass players aren't really.

— When do you think you developed greater range as a guitar player?

— I don't know. It's always been my first instrument. Just over the years playing more and maybe realizing you have a style that's yours, trying not to sound like other people but also being influenced by them and using other things. For some reason I was blessed a little bit by not copying people that well. When I would do it it just wouldn't exactly sound like it because there was enough of a variety of influences in there, maybe, and enough lack of skill at first to make it have its own sound. From the original idea the thing that really made Pavement sound like Pavement, beyond the vocals and the lyrics, which is maybe the most important thing in the long run — not that I would want to admit that — is the guitar tuning. Writing songs in these different guitar tunings is an idea that I would have learned from Sonic Youth, or at least the potential of it. Once I opened myself to that it made our songs sound a little bit different, even if they were standard songs. And we got some different tones. I've never gone away from that, so that was kind of the gateway to the Pavement sound. They're not particularly complicated tunings, but not standard. Taking some of the ideas of these open tunings but playing regular songs with them, so that it didn't really become just about the open tuning or about some avant-garde statement. More just like a tool to bring out different overtones and not sound like everybody else. That's probably what has led my guitar sound to be what it is more than anything else. Or why my solos sound like that. And it is pretty self-taught.

— I always think of Rattled by the Rush as your first really gnarly solo.

— Yeah. That does stand out. That's like a standard solo with a Marshall. I'd do it again if I could. Because that song was more rock, I guess. There were probably some quotation marks around the solo. But it's still a solo.

When I asked Scott Kannberg if he had a favorite Pavement record he said he had two — because they had two different drummers. He said Slanted and Enchanted was his favorite with Gary Young and Brighten the Corners was his favorite with Steve West. This struck me almost as revelatory. Of course I'm aware of Gary Young and his importance to the band — as a player, a recording engineer and an unhinged image-maker at their early shows. But when I listen to Pavement casually I don't break it down into different drummers. The concept of Pavement to me always includes Steve West. West lacked Young's surreal theatrics. He didn't do headstands or throw cabbage at shows. He also lacked Young's nimble chops. But he could make it through a show without falling over. He was up for the long-haul grind of Crooked Rain. He was up for goofing hugely in videos — his bit in Painted Soldiers is their funniest moment in the form. West brought a needed stability to Pavement. His friendships with Stephen and Bob locked in a tangible band chemistry.

— Bob and I would always tease ourselves, said West. — We'd say, well we're not very good but at least we're these guys, these freaks behind Stephen that people can see are having a good time and being enthusiastic. And it countermanded it when he wasn't. If people looked over at him and he was having a bad night they could look over at us and we were trying extra hard. I think that was part of the charm of the live show. We rarely practiced before our tours. I don't think we did it more than a dozen times in all the years that I was in the band. And even those were not real productive. Bob would always say we liked to start our tours in odd parts of the world where they'd never seen us before. So we could be bad and it wouldn't make the front pages.

I asked what it was like joining the band right as things were heating up.

— I tried not to think about it. I knew Pavement was a really popular underground band and I had really enjoyed their earlier work. And Bob was a longtime friend of mine and I'd worked with Stephen at the Whitney. When I joined it was between tours, of course, and that whole side of it — the whole publicity side and that kind of pressure and stuff — wasn't real apparent to me. It was just, Stephen and I would rehearse and kind of jam and then we went to Walleye's studio, this room where there was a drum set and a tape machine. It wasn't any producer-type thing. Walleye was there some of the time, making sure things were set up, and then he would go up to the music store and work. So it was very low-pressure. We got some victories out of that.

— And you worked on some Wowee Zowee songs

around that time too?

— Yeah. We recorded Crooked Rain that summer. And then I believe we went back before it was released and worked on more songs. And some of those songs ended up on Wowee Zowee. I remember Stephen being excited about some of those because they were a lot more off the wall and they had a different feel. So the thing about Wowee Zowee is it's got the dynamics of a harsher New York or punk kind of sound as well as the more southern sound that came out of Memphis. That's one of the reasons I always thought it was a unique record.

— What do you remember about going to Memphis to make it?

— Let's see. I guess we were there about two weeks. I remember we stayed in a really crappy hotel and I slept on the floor. I remember waking up and hearing — it was one of those suites where there was a door to another room — and hearing this couple in the other room making love and thinking, oh my god. I mean it was like right there and it was a really cheap motel. I remember Kannberg working on his songs. People trying really hard to produce a lot. There was a lot of prolificness going on. I heard the CD, the rerelease today for the first time and I was pretty amazed there were all those extra tracks and stuff on it.

— The record itself is long. Did you ever think it would have been better served by cutting it down some?

— No. We wanted to do something completely different. It felt right to do what we did. We had all those songs and instead of cutting it up — I know we probably talked about that and then we were just like no, put it together and see how it feels, this is bolder than anything else we could have done. I don't know if it sold any more or less than the previous records. It's hard to tell. It hasn't been hailed as the great one like Slanted and Enchanted and Crooked Rain have been. But it'll come around.

— So things were coming together fast in Memphis.

— Yeah. And there was a real good spirit in the band at that point. I don't think everyone was as burned out yet. Every band gets burned out. Not to say there's any negative thing about it. It's just one of those things that goes on with touring in a band and playing and being somewhat successful. Relationships have their high marks and their low marks. I think everyone at that time was in fairly good form and good humor and stuff, and real energetic.

— When did you notice that might have started to change?

— Hmm. Probably after Lollapalooza. Because that was such a rough experience for us. It was good and bad. Playing to the crowd walking away from you is hard. And realizing that we just weren't the Lollapalooza kind of band that was going to be successful for them. I mean it's a gradual thing when bands slowly turn away from each other, just like any marriage. There wasn't really any one moment or month or show.

— But Lollapalooza was a point where it started to feel more like work?

— Yes. It was kind of getting away from more of the Pavement, do-it-yourself, tour in a van thing. We toured in a van for Lollapalooza but it was for a different type of aesthetic that we hadn't really been a part of up until that point. We tried to shelter ourselves somewhat from the big record company-type stuff. But it hits you sometimes. And it was pretty apparent from the get-go, when they would have those people come to our shows and we'd have to have a meet and greet, that they really didn't — some of them seemed to get it but some of them seemed like these guys who had been with the label forever and were all about traditional classic rock. And we weren't. So it was obvious that we weren't gonna get the big push we probably needed. That could be as much our fault as it was their fault, you know. I don't think we always played the game as well or as cordially as we should have. But I don't think we really wanted to anyways.

— What was the songwriting process like after Wowee Zowee, when you and Stephen weren't living in the same town anymore?

— It was more like whoever was bringing the song to the table would come with the idea and we'd hash it out in the studio or some jam somewhere, at my place or wherever we were. And really it was Stephen and Scott crafting their own songs. We'd put in whatever input in the studio. But it wasn't like everyone said, all right we're gonna write a song and then everyone sat down at a round table.

— So maybe part of the reason Wowee Zowee has that feel is because you and Stephen were able to get together and goof around in your loft.

— Those New York songs, definitely. And then when we got to Memphis we had toured for a year together so that had more of a complete band feel. I think that's why Wowee Zowee has that dynamic and that dichotomy, just because we'd done all that touring together. Before that it was just fresh little me trying to figure out what to do with Stephen in Walleye's studio. That added some of the color to it. When you listen to Wowee Zowee you can hear the different quality of the recordings — the different rooms and drum sounds — from the different mics and compressors in the two studios, all put together over about a year.

— I talked to Doug Easley a couple months ago. After we hung up he called back and said, Bryan I forgot one thing, I always remember Steve West sitting there painting these little soldiers.

West laughed. — Yeah I think they thought I was a little nutty. You know after you've played your drums and you're just sitting around and everybody's talking and they're mixing or they're rerecording guitar tracks, there's a lot of down time. So you've got to do something besides just sit there and say yeah that sounds good over and over again. So I tried to keep myself busy doing other creative things too.

— He said he kept some of them in a shrine in his studio, I guess till it burned down.

— Yeah I know. That's too bad. I got some of those little dudes left. I don't know exactly where they are but maybe I could get his address and send him one. Put it in a bottle somehow. Stick a few in a bottle as a little diorama.

— Is that where Scott got the title for his song Painted Soldiers?

— Probably. And he also has that song Western Homes. He would call me *homes* sometimes. So maybe there's a dual meaning. When Scott would do his songs, at least when I recorded with him, it would pretty much be Scott and myself. I'd play the drums with him and he'd hash out his ideas, kind of like we did with Stephen sometimes, either with the whole group or earlier when I did the rehearsals for Crooked Rain. It was more of a partnership that way. You wouldn't have a room where all the band guys were sitting there playing together. Because Stephen didn't really know exactly how a song was gonna go and it was a lot easier to have a drummer and a guitar player with a guy singing. Some of the songs were done that way. Others were done with a full band, where we had hashed them out live or had more time to practice them together. Like Grounded. We'd played that a lot live.

— That's my favorite Pavement song.

— I think we did an earlier version of it and then rerecorded it at Easley.

— Yeah Walleye recorded that one. The Easley version, the slowed-down version is better, I think. Something about slowing it down really made that song.

— Really? Because I remember Stephen and I always talking about, yeah we should have made that one faster.

— Do you have any particular favorites on Wowee Zowee?

— Best Friend's Arm. I thought that one was really great. Extradition was really tough to figure out.

— How so?

— Well Stephen gave me a cassette of him just playing. And there's so many changes. That's kind of like his Royal Trux song. It seemed to go on and on. I remember going away with my wife for a week and listening to it over and over again just trying to memorize where it was gonna go, because it's not your average pop song. Pueblo's really good. Half a Canyon's great. Best Friend's Arm — if that was really produced it could have been a real big hit, I think. AT&T I like — and that could have been a really good song — but it just wasn't hitting. I don't even think I played drums on AT&T, I think Stephen did. Serpentine Pad, I like that too. Bob sings on that. Rattled by the Rush is another one that I thought was good but it's too slow for me now. But that's just me looking back thinking, I should have made them go faster!

One Sunday morning I left my pad and walked to Wowee Zowee cover artist Steve Keene's home/studio, about ten minutes away. Keene greeted me at the door and led me into a vast work space filled with hundreds of paintings instantly recognizable as his — bright slashes of color laid down in quick brush strokes, figures and scenes floating between representational and abstract. Beyond the work space was a living area. Keene's wife and their two young daughters were back there. Music was playing at a low volume. Keene and I sat on milk crates next to a stack of plywood panels. Keene looped wire through tiny holes in the panels, tied it into hangers, tossed the finished panels onto another stack. Later he would arrange a number of these in a fenced-off painting area and work on them simultaneously. We rapped about his early encounters with the Pavement guys. It began in Charlottesville Virginia. Keene and his wife had a radio show on WTJU, back when Bob Nastanovich, Stephen Malkmus and David Berman were working there. Keene had known Bob peripherally for a while. Bob had dated Keene's wife's little sister's best friend. The best friend's name was Chesley — as in Chesley's Little Wrists, one of Slanted and Enchanted's more fried-sounding numbers. Keene and his wife moved to New York in 89. They returned to Charlottesville two years later. In 93 they settled in New York for good. It was an exciting time. Malkmus and West were jamming in a loft down the street. Keene was making a ton of art. He'd honed this philosophy: do it like a rock band. Crank stuff out. Sell it for cheap. He's still doing it that way, making three hundred paintings a week.

— Is that the real number, three hundred?

— Yeah. I've sold over two hundred thousand — probably two hundred thirty thousand paintings in the past twenty years. So yeah, that's what I do. I think the direct link with Pavement — I mean we all had the same Fall records in Charlottesville and we played them on the radio and everything like that. The Wowee Zowee cover just sort of came about, I don't know why. I think at that time Malkmus almost wanted to delegate jobs to people. Maybe he was tired of being totally in control. Or maybe he wanted more spontaneity. It's still magic to me that I did it. It meant a lot to me because I'd known those guys for a long time.

— To watch their band get big must have been exciting.

— Yeah. I felt like I was friends with the Beatles. I was the number-one fan. It was thrilling. It was absolutely thrilling. It's not like I was close friends with those guys — I was more in awe of those guys — but we were all in the same circles. When I first started doing this people gravitated to the performance aspect of what I did. I was an exhibitionist too with my art. The way I do it, I mass produce it. Whenever I have a show I go to the gallery and I paint it there for people to watch. So I did a whole stack of probably fifty, sixty, seventy paintings on paper. And Malkmus picked the one that he wanted. The image is from some Time Life book on the middle east.

— I look at it and it seems like there's a poodle there.

— I think it's a goat.

— A goat. Okay. And two shrouded figures.

— Yeah. They're people sitting at an oasis someplace. It's odd — I can't really remember how it happened. Because I didn't really think it was going to happen. You know people say stuff and then it doesn't happen. Oh yeah, I like your pictures — but we decided to use Scott Kannberg's mom's painting or something. So I didn't want to be overly anxious. I tried not to — I kind of shut down when they asked me. Because it was a very big deal to me. I felt like this band of people — not band as in rock band — but this tribe of people came from Charlottesville and were attempting to conquer the world. And it kind of looked like it was going to happen for about a year and a half.

Keene got up and walked to the living area. He returned with a book.

— I don't think I've seen this picture — I don't think I've looked at this book since I did it. I copied it out of here.

It was a Life World Library title, The Arab World. Keene located the page and showed me the picture. The image I was seeing felt both intimately familiar and totally mysterious. For years I'd been carrying a reimagined version of it in my head. I used to sit with the record playing and just stare at the cover, wondering what if anything it was meant to convey.

— This is really strange for me to see, I said.

— I know, it's pretty weird, said Keene.

Two women in dark coverings, only their faces exposed, sit in an open-air structure. To their right is a small black goat with curled horns. Between them a young girl stands holding a baby. The caption reads: A midday rest is enjoyed by three Arab women and a goat on an arbor-shaded porch. Fellahin women often wear black robes over their other clothing.

— It's strange that I left out that figure right there.

He pointed to the girl in middle. — Normally I copy stuff. Why did I leave out the middle person?

— Is that how you usually work?

— Yeah. I always copy stuff. It's almost like hand-painted Rauschenberg or something. You grab stuff, you put it up, you copy it and you walk away. What was the coolest about the cover, they had it in a light box at Tower Records and I could see — and you can see on the CD too if you look at it — the staple marks where I'd stapled it onto a board to paint it. It was so funny to see my staple marks big.

Keene's visual association with Wowee Zowee went beyond the cover. He painted the backgrounds and set pieces of the interior portions of the Father to a Sister of Thought video. Those interiors were filmed in his Brooklyn loft. He painted stage sets used for tours for the record — visible in the Slow Century footage of Pavement's ill-fated Lollapalooza appearance in West Virginia, in which a sparse and largely hostile crowd pelts the band with mud. Malkmus leaves the stage in disgust after being struck in the chest. Kannberg stands at the edge of the stage and screams at the audience. Dirt bombs sail past him. He flips the crowd the double bird. He bares his ass.

— It really was my intention to mimic a band, said Keene. — The reason why I started selling my paintings like this was because whenever your favorite band would play a show at a bar they'd have a box of CDs or singles and start selling them. I used to go to places around here in New York and sell my paintings for two, three bucks. There was this place called the Thread Waxing Space. War Comet played there, this thing with Steve West, David Berman and Malkmus. And I got to hang my paintings up at that show. It was a huge space. It was like three times the size of this room. That was a really, really big help for me to get a lot of people turned on to my work like that. It was a thrilling time, it felt very communal. It was like you have your tribe of people and you try to create something. It felt like that right then. We were all still kind of fresh to New York and living off that adrenaline, like I'm in the city, I'm gonna do everything!

— Well it's like you said. For a year and a half Pavement —

— They changed the world.

— And then Wowee Zowee changed that in some way.

— Yeah. It made them another band to critique instead of a band to worship.

Friday afternoon a woman from my temp agency called. I hadn't heard from her in months. She asked if I'd be interested in a one-week proofreading gig starting Monday, twenty bucks an hour. My first thought was yes. The economy was in the shitter. I couldn't find work. My bankroll languished in the high two-figure range. I did a mental schedule check. The lone item next week: my second interview with Stephen Malkmus. Sorry, Ginger. I need time to prepare for and conduct the interview. I can't do it on a ten-minute break in a cubicle. I need silence and all kinds of fucking emotional space. No thanks, I said, but keep me in mind for other things. She never called again. The following week I called Malkmus.

— Scott said you guys tussled over the Wowee Zowee running order. He wanted to cut some of the stranger songs and have it just be the Easley tunes, I said.

— Yeah I can see him wanting that, said Malkmus. — And I can see it being good like that in a way. But it seemed to me like that would have just been another album. I wanted to have it more like the b-sides were actually on the record — what were considered b-sides at the time. Because people liked our b-sides anyway. Like the Minutemen's Double Nickels on the Dime, stuff like that. Longer records where you put out what you had and let it all hang out and weirder songs that were considered b-sides were actually just part of the band too. And there was more energy, I thought, in the songs that weren't from Easley. They were more spastic. There were some faster things in there. Like Best Friend's Arm and Flux = Rad. The Easley stuff is more laid back — not all of it but it's just kind of heavier.

— I always wondered about Easily Fooled. That song had been kicking around a while. It was on Peel Sessions and stuff. And then it ended up as a b-side on the Rattled by the Rush single. Which is surprising to me because it's such a great song.

— Yeah that's true. I don't know why we didn't put it on Wowee Zowee. It was done at the same time as Best Friend's Arm and Extradition. It was from that same time at Mark Venezia's studio. It is kind of catchy and Stones-y.

— Aside from Wowee Zowee did you do the cover art for the Pavement records?

— Yeah pretty much. And all the singles. I think at that time I just didn't have any good ideas and Steve Keene lived in the neighborhood and was a friend of the band. It was something we always thought about doing. It was the right time I guess. That Wowee Zowee painting he did, the colors and stuff, it looked a little like an album by this band Guru Guru, whose album cover I'd always liked. It's a German band, this album called Kanguru. The cover has kangaroos on it and I sort of appropriated that one to mix with Steve's, with the comic-book talk bubbles. Wowee Zowee sounded sort of like Guru Guru and it rhymed. So we picked that one and went with it. The other fonts, I don't remember what I was thinking. I did those with Mark Ohe. The inside thing was some drawing my grandma did in one of her phases.

— One of her phases was making art? Or that particular kind of art?

— That style, which was some kind of 40s-looking weird futurist drawing she did. She covered a lot of ground. That was probably around my apartment, something that she had given me. Then I made this writing thing. I remember it said Dick-Sucking Fool at Pussy-Licking School, which Bob made up. He probably doesn't want to own up to that. It was some stoner thing. I wrote that on there. I was just being kind of risqué or something. We thought that could be a good name for the album, like Cocksucker Blues by the Rolling Stones. If we could have called the album that, you know, that was an alternate title. Which would never be used. Maybe it would have been used by an Amphetamine Reptile band or some rock band back then. But Jesus Lizard wouldn't even do that. Maybe the Butthole Surfers would.

— What's your take on the meeting you guys had with Danny Goldberg?

— Danny was a pretty cool guy in general. He was powerful at the time. Matador followed him over to Warner Brothers, who did sort of a one-off with Pavement. They said, we'll pay a bigger advance and do more promotion, come over here, it's gonna be great. They did distribute it and promote it, I think. But it was an interim time. It was a new thing. Danny had just recently started and all of a sudden he was there in this high-up position. It's a venerable old company, Warner Brothers, with Mo Austin, who got the Kinks there. The Beach Boys were there for a while at the end. Van Dyke Parks, Randy Newman. But at that point Red Hot Chili Peppers and Green Day were two successful bands they had, along with Jane's Addiction and some other things I don't remember, like Candlebox — although I can't say that for sure. We flew out to Burbank. They have a campus out there that looks sort of like a California community college. Sixties architecture. It was kind of strange. We went to one meeting. There was another guy there, another older record guy. I can't remember his name. Not Mo Austin but someone like that, not quite as famous. We met him and we took a little walk around the place where there's posters of bands and people working at their desks. We went to Danny's office and it was all kind of — not adversarial but I was kind of skeptical of what it was gonna be like to be on this label. I didn't really expect to have a close connection with them. But they did listen to the CD, I know that. They had some comments about songs they liked and how they were gonna try and do these other songs for radio instead of Rattled by the Rush. They liked AT&T. But that was too sloppy and it was just me playing all the instruments. I didn't think that one was tight enough to be a single. They said, we might try to work that. They did some of that stuff and that was kind of it. It was a feeling-out vibe that was a little awkward, I remember. Danny feeling like he was brand-new in this chair and surprised that he was there in this powerful position. And the Matador guys feeling weird about it too. Chris and Gerard saying is this good, do you guys like this, is this gonna work? A couple times we did some promotional things. We met a few regional reps who gave us free CDs when we did an in-store. I remember a couple things like that, you know, in the Boston area or something. Regional rep-type people that we didn't have at Matador. But it came and went. I remember being aware that there was no single that was gonna take KROQ by storm, which was the standard way to try to become successful. Try to get on KROQ and people will like you and then it will bleed into other stations. Like the Offspring's Keep 'Em Separated, which was an indie record that really exploded. They spent a lot of money to make that happen — more than they would have spent for Pavement — but still.

— On the DVD you said you thought Rattled by the Rush and Father to a Sister of Thought sounded like hits. Were you just being funny or did you really think that?

Malkmus laughed. — Rattled by the Rush I thought was a really unique song for us. It had a lot of clever over-dubs and a different sound. I guess I didn't — I thought the riff was catchy. I thought it was a single, I don't know why. Father to a Sister of Thought, I was stoked with how it turned out with the pedal steel. It sounded better than I imagined it would when we recorded it. Like maybe from that time Mazzy Star's Fade Into You. That's about as big as it could ever be. It wasn't that big, of course. But from the label's mindset that would be their only hope.

It doesn't have a pretty girl just singing the same thing over and over again. But it has similar minor chords and not many chords.

— Have you ever been one to read your own press or follow reviews?

— When they come out normally we read them and try to get a sense of feedback. Some sort of validation of the work, at least that people listened to it and what they think. I read them to see what people are saying or what the placement is, like if you're gonna get a big feature in the NME or what's gonna go on. I'm kind of interested in that. I don't know about believing whether it's true or not.

— The reissue sort of screwed with my research. The Rolling Stone review is the only original Wowee Zowee review I could find. And that was a slam.

— Yeah that was real bad. I remember that being two stars or something. In his defense a little bit — whoever reviewed it — we had these cassettes that we handed out for people to hear first. They didn't give out CDs for review. I don't know if it was cheaper to do that or maybe we were just late. But all we had was an unmastered cassette. And it did sound pretty shitty. It sounded muddy. You could even not be a hater and want to like the band and think, this is dull sounding and doesn't go anywhere. After it got mastered it was brighter and sounded punchier, the way it was supposed to sound. Then again the guy could have just gotten it wrong. A lot of people disagree with him. I'm sure he would probably — provided he was a decent fan of Pavement — not think it was as bad as he did then. I would give him a second chance.

— Did you ever get sick of people calling you or the band slackers?

— Yeah well — in terms of the competition at that time, to not be a slacker the other things we could have been were like Jane's Addiction or the Offspring, tattooed LA people who were knowingly riffing on these classic rock or skate-surf archetypes. We were college-educated suburban kids. We didn't look like Dave Navarro. I don't know what else there was to really go on. I guess there was Seattle, Kurt Cobain and Nirvana. Kurt Cobain was a pretty big slacker, with heroin involved. But there was more of a story of economic hardship behind him, or divorced parents and pain from that. We didn't have that kind of pain really. We didn't riff on any of those things. Our band wasn't about that so I guess there wasn't much to say. We didn't make much of an effort to change it. At the time, coming out of the place that we came from, there was this big cynicism about the music industry and being successful in music. Dinosaur Jr and Sonic Youth, those kind of bands were the successful ones from that era. Those are basically slacker bands too. Sonic Youth just had some art-world New York guitars hiding the same basic slacker tenets. And Dinosaur had big giant guitars and solos. He was an ultimate slacker, J Mascis. It was just a big giant pool of slackerisms. It didn't really matter to us. Sometimes it got boring in England or something, once we got a little bigger, to keep getting asked about the movie Slacker or what a slacker was. Occasionally we'd say, we're not slackers, we tour a lot, we're really hard-working, would a slacker do that? No. What exactly is a slacker? Is it from that movie or is it just an uncommitted intellectual skeptic? People who just want to work in a record store their whole life and be kind of smart, like that movie of that book by Nick Hornby.

— I just remember there was this long article in the New York Times when your first solo record came out talking about how you were a big slacker and ironic and stuff. It was really appalling. I thought the time for that kind of analysis had long past.

— I was pretty much just into music and really excited about recording and layering things on records and making kind of classic-sounding albums. Like Scott would have been too. That's really what we were trying to do — take advantage of these situations that we didn't expect to find ourselves in. Which was having an audience and a voice in different places than we expected, coming from the 80s where Camper Van Beethoven was a huge band and Sonic Youth were massive. We were sort of built to not expect much success and therefore to seem sort of like slackers, because we weren't particularly ambitious to start with, more than just wanting to make cool records. It turned out that times were changing a little bit and there were lots of other seemingly suburban nerds coming to fill the void. They are the void now — Death Cab for Cutie or the Shins, in this town.

— I don't get too wrapped up in song meanings or anything but Grounded is my favorite Pavement song and over the years I've wondered what that one's about.

— Let's see. I couldn't even tell you. If I think about the lyrics . . . I don't even know what that's about anymore to tell you the truth. It sounds like it's vaguely about some Westchester County wealthy person, the son in some kind of 1990s Ice Storm scene. There's something there about somebody of privilege. There's a doctor, boys are dying on the streets. It's kind of cryptic. I know that some of the individual words and slang in it sounded important to me at the time. You know if I go through all those lyrics back then and how I wrote them it's really impossible for me to evoke what I was thinking. It was some kind of roll that I was on. It doesn't mean it was a good roll. Doing things without overthinking it too much and if it sounded cool that was good. I couldn't do that anymore. I just don't have the capability, whether that's good or bad. If you look at somebody like Bob Dylan, he did all this stuff and you don't know how he did it and he doesn't know how he did it. Maybe he was taking more speed than me.

— You're saying that's different from how you write songs now?

— I can't even imagine writing a song like that now, that's so cryptic. Maybe I can but I don't think so. You know it rhymes. So that's good. It's the same chords all the way through. Maybe that made it easier to write like that. It's called Grounded, which is something that happens — I don't really even know.

He laughed. — I'm sorry.

— That's all right. That's the danger of venturing too far into this stuff.

— I like the guitars in it a lot. The lyrics were something to try to sound sort of sincere and go along with the music. The bottom line was how the chords and some of the guitar made it feel and what that made me think of. But it kind of just happened then.

I asked Steve West if there was a time in Pavement he looked back on most fondly.

— Crooked Rain, Crooked Rain and Wowee Zowee, he said. — Because that was when it was really fresh to me and everyone was still enthusiastic. Everything before Lollapalooza.

I laughed. — Lollapalooza was the breaking point?

— It wasn't terrible. I mean we made good money. But it's not all about making money. We could have been out there playing to our own crowd, supporting Wowee Zowee in that way and it probably would have been more gratifying. But you know it's always good to do different things. What was Stephen's quote? He called me — I was in Virginia — and he said —

West flattened his voice, imitating Malkmus: — Yeah we're gonna do it. It's just another nail in the coffin but we're gonna do it. It doesn't matter.

— But thank god that happened, said Kannberg.

— Otherwise I wouldn't have been able to buy a house. Lollapalooza basically bought everybody in Pavement a house. They paid us like twenty grand a show. We were worth maybe four and a half.

He laughed. — It was the easiest thing ever to do. There'd be three shows a week. And we didn't have a big bus, we had two little minivans. None of our expenses went toward giant buses. It was really fun. Playing the shows wasn't that fun because I don't think Steve was really into it. The rest of us had a great time. Lollapalooza carried all of our equipment and set it up every day. We made them buy us a ping-pong table and set it up every day. It was hilarious.

— You said you wanted Wowee Zowee to be a tighter record and mentioned the songs you wanted to cut. You also said listening to it now you see why it works. Was it just a matter of living with the record for a while?

— I always knew the way it was presented it was more like — I hate comparing it to the White Album because I don't think the Beatles thought they were making what that record ended up being. But you have to compare it with something and that's what I compare it to. We were pretty overwhelmed at that time because we'd been doing so much. Then we went and recorded everything we had and what came out was a little messy. It's almost like when a band, after everything's all said and done, they put out an outtakes record. It almost felt like that to me. It was so different from our other records. Even the song material was different. There's country songs. There's weird Captain Beefheart-y songs. Every song had a certain vision to it. Every song was self-contained.

Whereas on our other records you can see how the songs fit together.

— Do you think there's a greater appreciation for the record now?

— Oh definitely. Definitely. But you have to think of it in the context of our whole career. If that was the only record we ever put out I don't think it would have been as significant. I also don't think it's the same for a fan hearing it for the first time now. I don't know if it creates the same kind of feeling as people back then hearing it after Crooked Rain. Some kids today say to me, Wowee Zowee is so great, so much better than your other records.

— It's a very free album, said Bob. — I think Stephen's solo work really proves that he's an avid fan of pretty far-out, experimental music. He always has been. His radio show in college was fifty percent unlistenable. I think having to play those Crooked Rain songs over and over again probably in a way made him sick. They ended up sounding like bubblegum to him. So I think he wanted to get back to the haphazard ways of Slanted and Enchanted. That's why some pretty weird songs ended up on Wowee Zowee. They weren't weird to us. It just all sounded like Pavement to us. The only Pavement songs that I don't — a lot of people like these songs but I just don't because they don't seem like Pavement to me are songs like Major Leagues and Carrot Rope. They don't sound like Pavement to me. Just about everything else does.

— A lot of people say that about Terror Twilight generally.

— That was just a whole different type of album. Wowee Zowee represents probably the happiest era of Pavement. We were feeling good about the fact that everybody was making a living off it and everybody had done the right thing in putting down what they were doing in 92 to devote their lives to this band. Everybody had a role and everybody got along. It was an upbeat time, at least within the shell of the band. We loved our crew. We had the same crew for years and it was a very tight-knit group of people. In some ways we felt like a little juggernaut. The dissolution of the band would have begun during the making of Terror Twilight. There was the feeling that Stephen was real frustrated with us, I guess mainly due to lack of musicianship.

— So there was perhaps a shift in his thinking, from wanting to get back to that looser sound to moving on to something more accomplished?

— I think Stephen felt that he was better musically than the four of us, that we were holding him back and that he wanted to play with better players. That came to a head during Terror Twilight. That's Pavement's most singer-songwriter-type album. Stephen and Nigel Godrich really made that record. Stephen was pretty dissatisfied the whole year and I think more than anything else he didn't want to dislike me or dislike any of us. He was just frustrated. The sad thing was, it was like the demise of just about every other band. It was typical. And that was the most embarrassing thing about it.

— People make a big deal out of the Pavement dynamic and that being what broke up the band, said Ibold. — But it was a more subtle thing than people imagine it to have been. That's not to say it wasn't a serious issue. I think that we were lucky to get along as well as we did. Everyone gets along quite well still, I would say.

— Do you ever get tired of people asking you if Pavement will reunite?

— I've got to say that I don't because it's nice to hear that people still care about the band. I think it's amazing I'm even talking to you on the phone about an album that came out such a long time ago. I think it's great that people are still psyched about it. It makes me feel better about what we did. Because I still really like all of that stuff and I keep worrying that it will become dated and therefore I will be dated.

He laughed. — And it's crazy because a lot of the people that are interested in this stuff were too young to have seen the band when it came out. It reminds me of my interest in, I don't know, Captain Beefheart or something that I didn't get to see. There also have been a lot of reunions lately. People expect every band that's broken up that had somewhat of a following to get together and do a reunion tour now. I think that works against the possibility of a Pavement reunion. We like the idea of doing something surprising or special and it becomes less special the more you hear about other bands doing it. At the same time all these people that have never seen the band, it'd be fun to play for them.

— I said something to that Warners guy, said Malkmus, — the guy whose name I can't remember. I was like, you know it's okay if we don't get the radio thing because

Wowee Zowee's a great record and it'll sell as a catalog thing because it's a critical success — I didn't say critical success — but it's a great record and it'll keep selling. You think that when you're a young band, that you'll make a great record and people will keep buying it through time. But that's not how it matters to a record label. It's all now. You have to try to sell a million now. Like White Light/White Heat didn't do any record labels any good even though it's a classic record that people listen to still. The record label doesn't care about that. They do for Dark Side of the Moon or Paul's Boutique. Those keep selling but they sold so many at the start too. Anyway I was a little delusional about that.

— Of course if Pavement became the most popular band in the world their core fans wouldn't have liked them. So it's a vicious circle, said Lombardi. — But it helped them in terms of their legend to a degree, never having a platinum record. They never sold as many records as they should have. I mean how many times has Slanted and Enchanted or Crooked Rain been named the most important indie rock record of the 90s, or of all time? Over and over and over again. Well if that's the case then shouldn't they have sold a couple million records? So I guess it's that underdog mentality too. Pavement made great fucking records and they didn't compromise. It feels good to like them.

I was on the phone with a woman from Nielsen SoundScan. She dished Pavement sales figures as of June 2009. The original version of Slanted and Enchanted sold 152,000 copies. The reissue sold 106,000. Crooked Rain, Crooked Rain: 246,000. The reissue: 75,000. Wowee Zowee: 129,000. The reissue: 32,000. Brighten the Corners: 154,000. The reissue: 16,000. Terror Twilight — reissue forthcoming — sold 104,000 copies, more than I would have guessed. I don't know what any of this means. I'm way past caring. Three years have blown by since I started planning this book. I began with a head full of theories, arguments, assertions. I filled two legal pads with notes. In the end I used almost none of it. It blew away in the wind —

But I am still sitting on the floor of this room. Next to the record player is a bourbon on ice. I drop the needle on the vinyl, the first of three sides. There's a momentary pause but the pause is not empty. There's slight hiss and crackle as the needle works into the grooves. I lay back and close my eyes. All that you've seen and done and written and remembered. Yet everything not coming through your speakers at this moment is entirely beside the point —

The first note of the first song is a lonesome plucked E string. Sad tinkling piano. Faint exhalation of disgust or defeat. It jumps to A. Malkmus sings *there is no . . . castration fear*. We Dance begins with a Freudian joke then shifts to the kind of muted longing he does so well. *We'll dance, we'll dance but no one will dance with us in this zany town.* What appealed to me from the start were those hidden depths. Where some saw only sarcasm or detachment I saw slyly masked fear, joy, sadness, lust. *You can't enjoy yourself, I can't enjoy myself . . . maybe we could dance together.* Slow fade on this half-hopeless suggestion. Then the KROQ smash that never was. I bought the Rattled by the Rush single in Washington DC early February 98. I was visiting my father. We had long been estranged. His second wife had died. We'd gone to the memorial service together. I hadn't wanted to go, hadn't wanted to visit him at all. I'd been listening to Wowee Zowee obsessively and knew Rattled well. *Worse than your lying, caught my dad crying.* I didn't know the b-side, Easily Fooled, one of Pavement's best songs. Stephen Malkmus must be a merciless self-editor. Over the years he's discarded great song after great song. He wanted to ax Summer Babe from Slanted and Enchanted — a song plenty of people would kill to have written. Scott Kannberg intervened. The song opens the record. They played it live for as long as they were a band. I listened to the Rattled single in my dad's sterile apartment. Easily Fooled shuffled along to the bridge. *Everybody needs a home, takes centuries to build, seconds to fall.* My father and I sitting there listening to those lines. I'd like to see more of you, he said. How about some ice cream? he said. He got up and went into the kitchen. The guitar solo in Rattled snakes through your brain. The ice in your drink has melted, the whiskey feels good in your throat. A thought bubbles up but fails to cohere, something about music being put to tape in a room in Memphis or New York, lost to the atmosphere, falling through time. Snow like a star shower flying out of the darkness. You squint through the windshield at the snow-covered road. You can only go twenty, twenty-five maximum. Occasionally you pass a house, its windows darkened. It's after midnight. There are no other cars out. The cold of this night envelopes you as you make your way home. Blackout on the stereo. *Count to ten . . . and read . . . until . . . the lights begin to bleed.* The guitar line at the end conjures an early fall day, a taste of cold on the air but the leaves haven't changed yet. The smell of black walnuts hangs heavy in the dusk. That's part of it too, that subtle tension in his lyrics, a feeling that time pushes you forward and you have no choice but to move on but maybe someone you left behind was really worth holding on to, so many people drop in and out of your life, how can you ever know for sure? Brinx Job is the first of the far-out numbers. A classic Pavement prankster jam, in and out in a minute and a half. Dig the last fifteen seconds in which our heroes become gremlins tearing at the plane's engines mid-flight. In the distance a voice counts *three four*. Grounded shimmers to life. The door

to the record for me. I stood listening to the guitar intro
at the Intersection first with vague curiosity then as if in
a trance. The song builds slowly, adding and stripping
away layers. The doctor is leaving for some summer
holiday. He owns a sedan. Never complains when it's hot.
The strings bend pre-chorus. Harmonics flash like blue
sparks. Early one December morning I walked out of a
house. The Kalamazoo streets were quiet and still. I'd
stayed up all night with Chrissy. We started out watching
a cable documentary about the Titanic. All that winter
the doomed ship was the rage. We went up to her room
and lay on her bed. We held each other and talked. I kept
thinking I would leave but I didn't and then it was dawn.
Chrissy was still dating Plastic Man but that would end
soon and she and I would be together. For now it was
just me on McCourtie Street walking home. I put on
my headphones, pressed play on my Walkman. Brinx
Job ended and Grounded began and the world looked
dazzling, so bright and strange, like the light had spilled
out of me and wanted back in. *Boys are dying on these
streets*. I used to imagine he was saying my name at that
part coming back in from the breakdown, the drums and
guitars build, listen closely you'll hear *Buh-ryan*. There
were times when I almost convinced myself it was true.
Pavement have a few real barn-burners in their catalog.
Serpentine Pad is one of them, a bracing dose of punk
rock. Malkmus in punk-brat mode railing against snoring
and corporate integration, Bob on the chorus sounding
gloriously unhinged —

The questions are the questions. They never get
answered. Like what does this mean, why can't I control

it, where oh where in the motherfucking hell are we
bound? I walked to the kitchen, poured another drink.
Sometimes the days are so long and sad. Other times
even the Con Ed bill winks cheerfully. Life is a marvel of
sweet times and pals. I returned to my room and flipped
the record. I heard the music a second or two before it
actually began —

We lurch forward drunkenly, holding the walls for
balance. After a pause the soundtrack to some stoned film
noir. There's this great line in Motion Suggests Itself,
the second verse, *captivate the senses like a ginger ale rain*
delivered in a hush over a droning keyboard that haunts
the song. The atmosphere so humid you almost long for
that rain, almost feel the first drops cooling your skin.
Dueling guitars give way to a lone languorous solo, a
creak like insects in a moonlit marsh. But really Motion
Suggests is the candle. Father to a Sister of Thought is
the flame. My last summer in Kalamazoo I lived in an
apartment with no furniture. Paul and Trish had moved
out and taken everything with them except a recliner and
an old TV. I set the TV on a piano bench in the empty
living room. Every night I stayed up late watching the
talk shows. Chrissy was in Europe for a month. I was
making out with her friend. I felt guilty all the time but
couldn't stop myself. I thought my life was boring and
wanted to be someone else. I drove around Kalamazoo
trying to memorize the landscape, missing the city ter-
ribly even though I was still there. *I'm too much, I'm
too much comforted here*. In a way Father to a Sister of
Thought is the sequel to Range Life, broadening the
latter's sun-bleached palette and dreams of escape with

lonely pedal-steel guitar. But where the guy in Range Life can't settle down the guy in Father to a Sister knows he'll never go. Then the tune shifts abruptly, the pedal steel cuts out, an angular fuzzed-out riff ends the song. Barely time to take a breath before Extradition blooms and we make our w-w-way way far away. Less than a minute in: hang gliding, soaring over the wasteland. Scan the horizon. Tell me what you perceive. Another dismal truth maybe. Like you have no more right to exist than a paperclip does. You're either bent-out alone jabbed into a cubicle wall or strung together with two dozen others to be played with while your creator raps with some dame on the phone. *Tonight we interact like separate worlds, spoken barriers you hurl.* I am not the same person who clawed at your prom dress, breadstick grease on my tux, an Olive Garden gift certificate in my hand. No I'm a private investigator now. I stare into people's dark hearts for a living. Don't ask what I find there. You'll learn soon enough. I captured the moment of your ultimate ignominy using a penny glued to the sidewalk and a tele-photo lens. Funny that Steve West thinks Best Friend's Arm could have been a hit. I mean it's catchy and all but aside from *keep it under your best friend's arms* — which comes at the end after the song settles down — I'm able to make out only eight words in the flurry of vocals: *come on, let it go, take it off.* Even the verse hook is a mystery to me. Over the years I've heard it as *I can see, I can see* and *I concede, I concede.* But there's a *z* sound in there so it could be a foreign word, German perhaps. There have been plenty of nonsense hits — Tutti Frutti, Brimful of Asha, Song 2 — but usually those have at least one clear

phrase propelling them. Everyone said Blur wanted to be
Pavement on that last one. If that's the case something
crucial got lost in translation. Even so, their self-titled LP
is the best thing Blur ever did. Has it ever saved me from
drowning or slashing my wrists? No. Four notes up, the
same four notes down. Someone you've been wanting
to see opens the door. *Come on in*. A rush of fine feeling
swells in your chest. Grave Architecture is a fun one to
sing along with while driving, a rare occurrence now that
I live in New York, where music is experienced mostly as
a private distraction beamed straight into your head or as
just another fucking thing your computer can do. Maybe
this is true everywhere. We live in a detestable era. I'd
be the first to sign up for time-travel experiments. Doc
Brown, warm up the flux capacitor. I'd risk being shot by
terrorists to live in a pre-cellphone age. Here's another
one that informed my early impressions of the city. The
wind blew through the midtown canyons. Central Park
was a wonder in the autumn light. The air was scented
with smoke from the food carts. Horses drew carriages
along the path. *Stroll past the strip, is it old, am I clipped,
am I just a phantom waiting to be gripped around on shady
ground?* Halfway through they pull the rug out from
under us. They make thunder happen. Then everything
begins again fresh and new just like we've heard it would
since about middle school. One or two false endings
later Grave Architecture closes with an instrumental
version of the timeless childhood taunt Malkmus would
later employ in his read of the *wave to the camera* line
on the Brighten the Corners song Stereo. I love the big
inhalation that begins AT&T. I love the first line, *maybe*

someone's gonna save me. I love the idea of a heart made of gravy. I love the primitive drum fill on *room service calls.* I love the high guitar that runs under the second verse. I love how Malkmus alludes to Random Falls, the very studio he's recording in, and how that name calls to mind both disorder and wonder, water hurtling over large high cliffs. I love the way he shouts GO! into the chorus. I love the chorus itself, *whenever whenever whenever I feel fine I'm gonna walk away from all this or that*, the implication being that not feeling fine at the moment is okay, there's really no rush, whenever you get your shit together or feel better, that's the right time to move on. I love the line *come along, lads,* half-buried in a momentary blur. *One two three GO!* Tonight the lights blaze up and down Second Avenue. The sidewalks teem with beauteous mobs. On Ninth Street two foxy women pass trailing perfume and smoke. Dimly you hear their voices, brief laughter, and then they are gone. One life, one face, always hides multitudes. No one ever laughs the same way twice. I showed up here tonight hoping to see you. I wanted to tell you I had a dream that we kissed. We were standing in a hallway, the party noise was crazy, I touched your arm with a trembling hand. The dream was so real I woke in the street covered by a quilt of old love notes. Some neighborhood kids were lighting the best ones on fire, throwing them into the starless sky —

My father returned with a bowl of ice cream. He ate it. The spoon clinked as he scooped up the last melted bits. He set the empty dish on the coffee table. Boy that really hit the spot, he said. He put in a CD of Eric Clapton's greatest hits. He started talking about his dead wife. A moment later he paused. He looked away. The room was dimly lit but I thought I saw tears in his eyes. Clapton sang *I don't wanna fade away*. I retreated to the bathroom and stared through the mirror into history. I touched the panic button in my teeth with my tongue. I rematerialized in a record store in Broad Ripple Indiana. I was flipping through the used vinyl, saw a copy of Wowee Zowee and paused. Something compelled me to take it out of the bin. It was a double LP with a gatefold cover. I removed the second record from its sleeve and put it on the turntable. When I lifted the needle the record started to spin —

Pavement like to sex it up sometimes too and Flux= Rad has a sinister sexual quality, a jittery riff, an anxious seducer speaking close to your ear saying he doesn't wanna let you go. Then in the next verse dropping all ambiguity, telling you straight-up no he's not going to. His tautly controlled voice shoots into hysterics. Is this what it's like to be loved, a bass drum thumping up and down your spine? A dark room with a bed with cool sheets and a fan going? That's what I would long for at three a.m. in the paper mill as far away you slept bathed in murderous dreams. I stood with a hose spraying paper pulp and cockroaches into the grates. Burning oil dripped into my hair. I walked to the break area and bought a sausage-gravy-filled biscuit from the vending machine. I zapped it in the microwave for two minutes on high. Tony Buck was there. He asked what I was studying in school. English, I said, writing. What do you wanna be, a author? he asked. I guess so, yeah, I'm not too sure it'll pay the bills though, I said. Paid

Hemingway's bills, said Tony, and he blew his head off anyway. We laughed. I finished my biscuit. I walked out to the loading dock and stared at the night. One of the times I saw Pavement at Irving Plaza in 99 Malkmus said something like, this song's old but it's still good, well not the lyrics maybe but the music's still good, don't listen to the lyrics. Then they played Fight This Generation, which is more like two and a half songs, the first a stream-of-consciousness dirge haunted by Sibel Firat's cello, the second a faster almost paranoid-sounding number whose keyboard wavers like a police siren under the words *fight this generation*, a mantra. The last minute or so is as close as Pavement gets to funk, a steady shuffling bass line, a tight beat punctuated by drunken keyboard stabs and wild squiggly guitar. I always thought the title was Malkmus's way of deflecting some of the slacker bullshit. You think I'm a part of this but I am not. The whole deal was born in a conference room anyway. Let's put Eddie Vedder screaming on the cover of Time with a probing essay about the bleak future inside. Well you were right. It made everyone feel special. I called my mom and told her punk rock was changing my life. And look at us now, twenty years later, twenty light years from hip, connoisseurs of a thing known to marketers as content. Passionate readers of ceaseless flickering ads. Along the way there were intimations of mortality, easy enough to ignore. What has changed, what has changed? We won't die today and maybe not ever. Kennel District burns with a dazzling phosphorescence that's all the more remarkable for the song's simplicity, just the same three notes in a drop-D progression played over and over for three minutes, perfect pop song length. You could be in a city walking the streets slightly buzzed squinting into the headlights and rush of faces — or in the country gazing heavenward with stars in your teeth. Either way you feel a tug of regret. *Why didn't I ask, why didn't I ask?* Scott Kannberg pulled a neat trick later, moving the Kennel District chords down a step, inverting the progression on the verses and laying on some Byrds jangle. The result was Date with IKEA, another one of his gems. You could wash your face at night and slip into bed without a clue as to what transpired that day or wake the next morning feeling vaguely thankful you still exist before remembering with a shiver all that's left to be done. I don't wanna be young again but jesus I sure as fuck don't wanna get any older. Is there a third option? Yes but it takes a certain type of individual. Curtis, Cobain. You are not like them. You're too fond of that sweet ache, the little electric moment pre-kiss. In a small room in a law office at 120 Broadway I had a temp gig entering lawyers' timesheets into a database, moving only three fingers on my right hand. Information Center, I said whenever I answered the phone. During slow times I imagined it was all a movie. I leaned back in my chair and stared at the ceiling as a camera filmed from above. The song on the soundtrack was always Pueblo. The opening guitars and first verse telegraphed a pleasant ennui. The piercing note that drives the chorus hinted at deeper agonies. I never found a way to end the scene, it merely drifted on like the middle part of the song. *When you move you don't move you don't move.* The vocals at the end of Pueblo are some of my favorite on the record even though it's not clear what if anything is being said. Probably the voice there is meant only to compliment the swirling guitars that dominate the mix. Malkmus has been endlessly and rightly praised for his linguistic gifts. But he's equally adept at creating moments of pure feeling using few if any discernible words. As he does at the start of Half a Canyon, a drawn-out screech culminating in the delightfully world-weary *aw shit, baby*. Later he unleashes a series of terrifying screams. *Oh my god I can't believe I'm still going*. Only for another moment. We've arrived at the end. Twin visions of California. A desert redness falling over Spahn Movie Ranch. Setting out under cover of night for a creepy-crawl in the Hollywood Hills. In another view wave after wave of strip malls ripple out from a dying town center. Living room windows flash TV glow. *Western homes are locked forever, the new frontier is not that near*. Down these streets with English country manor names we'll skateboard. On pale lawns we'll huddle and plan our escape. There is no escape. We were fools to believe it. Yet there never was anyone more hopeful than me, bounding through the static, a song on my lips. Unchain your heart, honey. I like you. I am en route —

Also available in the series

Acknowledgments

Thank you: David Barker, Paul Bayer, Nils Bernstein, Brooklyn Writers Space, Sam Brumbaugh, Trish Chappell, Dianne Charles, Gerard Cosloy, Doug Easley, Bryce Goggin, Danny Goldberg, Mark Ibold, Scott Kannberg, Steve Keene, Dan Koretzky, John Liberty, Chris Lombardi, Anna Loynes, Stephen Malkmus, PJ Mark, Rian Murphy, Bob Nastanovich, Matthew Perpetua, Wendy Raffel, Jacob Slichter, Richard VanFulpen, Mark Venezia, Steve West, Karla Wozniak.

BUYING BOOKS IN BOOKSTORES IS COOL.